Science 4

for Christian Schools®

"Thus saith the Lord the maker thereof, the Lord that formed it, to establish it; the Lord is his name; Call unto me, and I will answer thee, and shew thee great and mighty things, which thou knowest not."
Jeremiah 33:2-3

Dawn L. Watkins

NOTE:

The fact that materials produced by other publishers are referred to in this volume does not constitute an endorsement by Bob Jones University Press of the content or theological position of materials produced by such publishers. The position of the Bob Jones University Press, and the University itself, is well known. Any references and ancillary materials are listed as an aid to the student or the teacher and in an attempt to maintain the accepted academic standards of the publishing industry.

SCIENCE 4 for Christian Schools®
Second Edition

Dawn L. Watkins

Produced in cooperation with the Bob Jones University Department of Science Education of the School of Education, the College of Arts and Science, and Bob Jones Elementary School.

ISBN 0-89084-433-X (hardbound)
ISBN 0-89084-622-7 (softbound)

15 14 13 12 11 10 9 8 7

Contents

History of the Moon

"And God made two great lights; the greater light to rule the day, and the lesser light to rule the night: he made the stars also." *Genesis 1:16*

The Moon's Beginning

Science can be defined as "information gained by using our senses." *Faith* means "holding beliefs without seeing, hearing, tasting, smelling, or touching the proof of them."

When the moon came into being, were there any people there to get facts through their senses? Then do all our ideas about where the moon came from rest on science or faith? What anyone believes about the beginning of things rests on faith, not science. Hebrews 11:3 says that *"Through faith* we understand that the worlds were framed by the word of God."

Theories on the Moon's Origin

People who accept the Bible believe that God made everything. They call God's description of how things began the *Creation Model.* Those who disregard the Bible believe instead that everything got here by itself. They call this description of how things began the *Evolution Model.* Evolutionists try to guess what events caused things like the moon. Following are three guesses made by evolutionists about how the moon began.

The Break-Away Theory

Some scientists believe that the earth was once like a rolling, boiling ball of lava such as volcanoes spit out. As the sun's gravity pulled on the earth, a large lump of soft rock formed on one side of it. Because the earth was spinning fast, this lump broke away and shattered into tiny pieces. Then the pieces pulled back together to make the moon. The "hole" left in the earth, they say, became the Pacific Ocean.

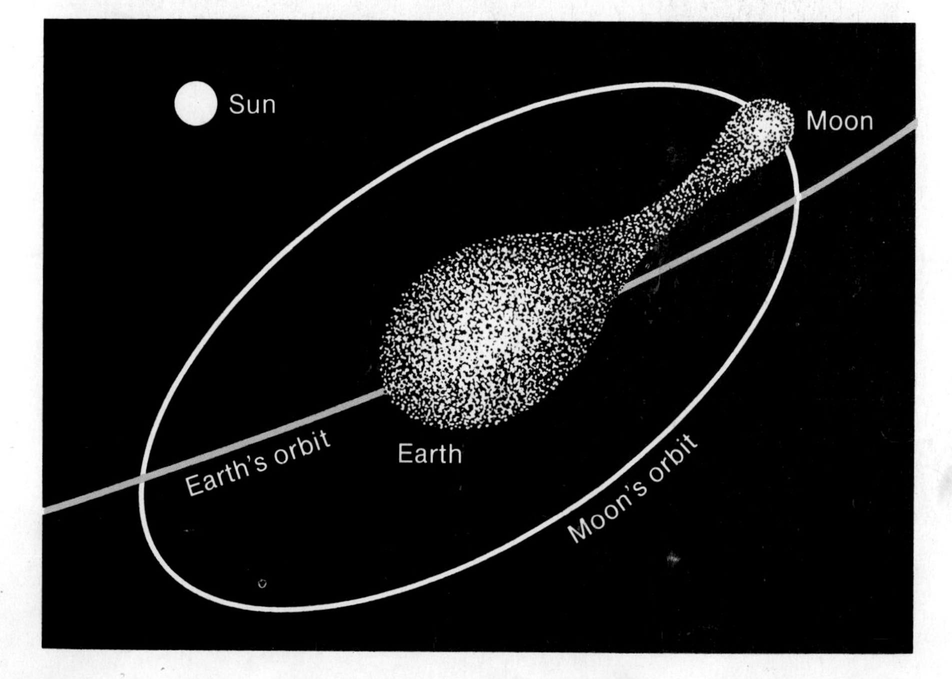

See if you can find any problems with this theory. Look for a moment at the chart. The column labeled *density* shows how the mass of one cubic foot of earth compares to one cubic foot of the moon. Is the earth's density the same as the moon's density? Shouldn't they be the same if the moon came from the earth? Check the other columns. Do the earth and the moon have the same rocks and minerals? What do you think about this Break-Away Theory? Does it seem that the moon could have come from the earth?

	EARTH	MOON
Density	5.52 gms/cm^3	3.34 gms/cm^3
Igneous Rocks:	mostly granite	no granite
Minerals		
Armalcolite	not found on earth	found on moon
Tranquillityite	not found on earth	found on moon
Pyroxferroite	not found on earth	found on moon

The Capture Theory

What do you think of when you hear the word *capture?* Gangsters or pirates? To "capture" usually means to seize someone or something from another place. Those who believe the Capture Theory think that the moon once had its own path around the sun like the nine planets. But when the earth's path came close to the moon's path, the earth captured the moon with its pull of gravity.

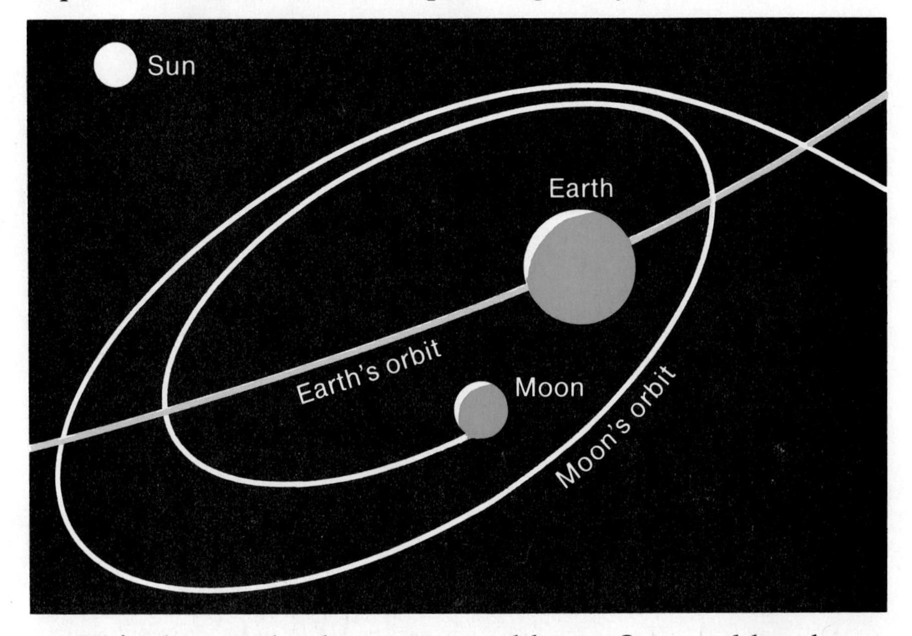

This theory also has some problems. One problem has to do with which has more "stuff," the earth or the sun. The more "stuff" something is made of, the more pull of gravity it has. The sun has 333,400 times more material than the earth. So which has the greater pull of gravity? The sun does. If the moon was once on its own path around the sun, then how could the earth (distances remaining the same) capture the moon away from the sun? Could some big accident have helped the earth capture the moon? The solar system is so orderly that such an accident does not seem possible.

Another problem with the Capture Theory has to do with the speed of the moon. If the moon had been traveling slowly when it came near the earth, it would have crashed into the earth and broken up into small pieces. If it had been traveling really fast, it would have zoomed off into a new path around the sun. It would have been a rare chance indeed that the moon was traveling at just the right speed to get captured in one piece by the earth.

Furthermore, this capture might have caused great heat on earth. Some scientists believe that it would have made so much heat that part of the crust would have melted. But when they look at the earth's materials, they find no evidence that anything like that ever happened.

The Condensation Theory

The word *condense* means "to make thicker." What are scientists who believe this theory thinking? They think that the earth and the moon were both formed from the same cloud of dust and gas. They assume that the dust and gas condensed, or thickened, to make a solid earth and moon.

You probably see a problem with this theory right away. How did the gas and dust gradually come together? Have you ever heard of it happening before? You have already seen that the earth and moon have different densities and different rocks and minerals. If the earth and the moon formed from the same gas and dust, should they not be more alike? Do you think this theory is reasonable?

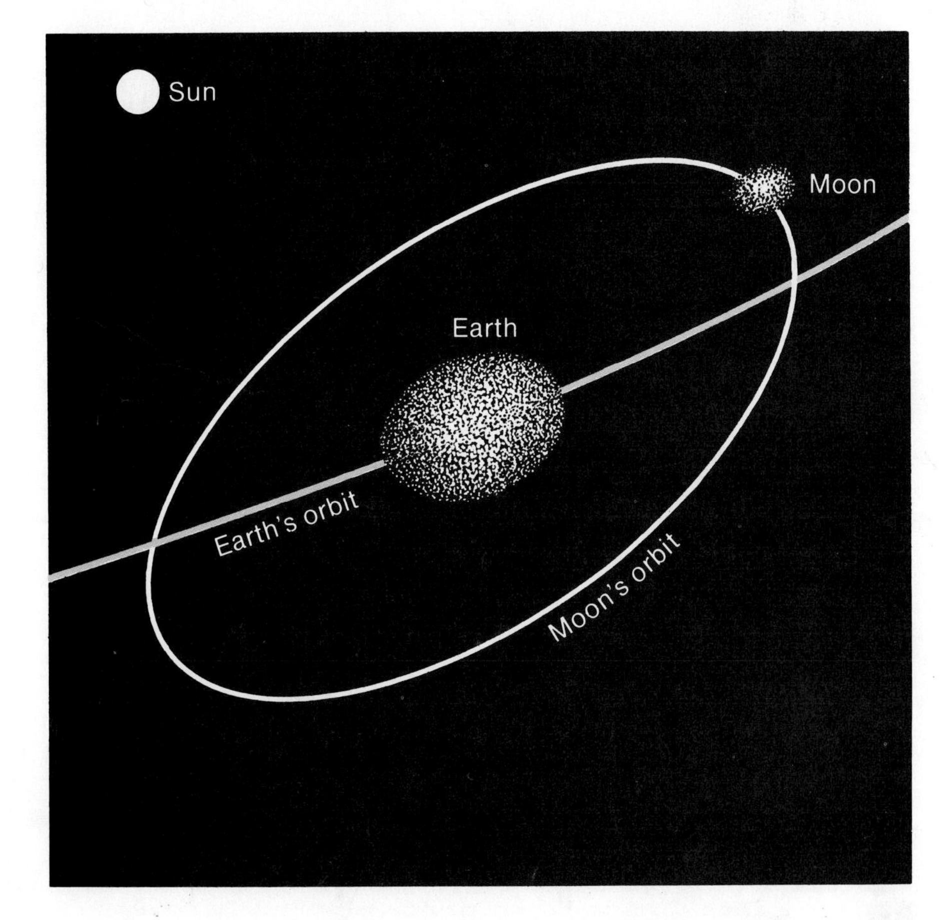

The Biblical Record of the Moon's Origin

The three theories just discussed are some scientists' guesses about how the moon began. But Christians do not have to guess how things began. The Bible not only tells us that God made the lights in the heaven but also that He made them out of nothing. The last part of Hebrews 11:3 says "that things which are seen were not made of things which do appear." No material thing existed until God spoke.

The creation of the moon, like everything else, took place immediately. Psalm 33:9 says, "He spake, and it was done." The moon sprang into being in an instant, at God's command.

The Age of the Moon

"How old is the moon?" This question has puzzled scientists for centuries. Evolutionists assume that the moon is billions of years old because their model requires great spans of time for things to happen by chance. But creationists believe the moon is much younger, perhaps only 10,000 years old.

Activity on the Moon

One trait of youth is activity. Many people have observed signs of activity on the moon, such as streaks of light flashing and small areas changing color. Such activity is called *transient lunar phenomena.* Some people have written books telling about their observations. If such changes are taking place on the moon today, is the moon more likely old and dead or young and active?

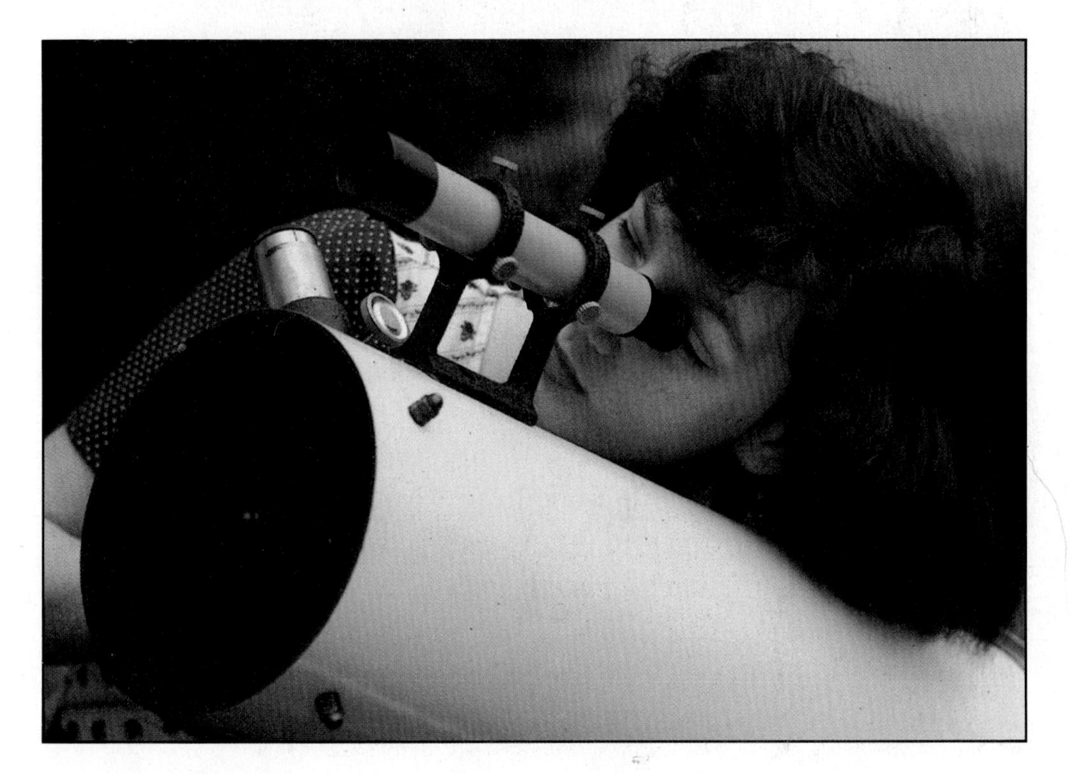

Dust

Each year dust from comets and material from the sun settle onto the earth and moon. On the earth, this dust finds its way to the oceans. On the moon, it settles in the low areas. Scientists have figured out how much dust builds up each year on the moon. If they assume that it has always been the same amount each year, then they can calculate how much there is with the following formula:

amount of build-up per year × number of years = amount of dust

Suppose you figured out that 0.0001 inch of dust gathers on the moon each year. An evolutionist would multiply 0.0001 inch per year times one billion (1,000,000,000) years. And he would say that the moon had one hundred thousand (100,000) inches of dust! But a creationist would multiply .0001 inches per year times 10,000 years. And he would say that the moon has one inch of dust. How much dust did the astronauts discover when they were on the moon? They found only a very thin layer. Does the moon seem to be old or young?

Distance

Another reason to believe that the moon is young is its distance from the earth. Scientists have found that the moon is getting farther away from the earth each year. They can measure how much farther away it is getting each year. Evolutionists could multiply the distance that the moon is moving away by one billion years (the age they think the moon is). This would tell them that the moon should be farther away than it is. Could the moon be as old as the Evolution Model requires it to be?

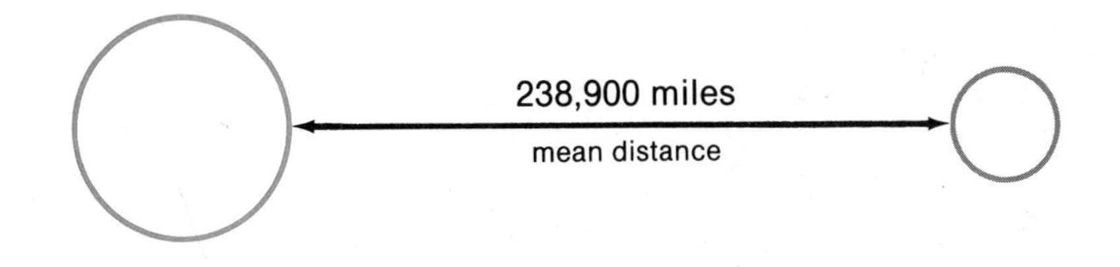

The Purpose of the Moon

Have you ever wondered why God made you? Or why God made anything? God made you and all things for His own glory (I Chronicles 16:28, Romans 11:36, and I Corinthians 6:20; 10:31). But how can something like the moon bring glory to God? Read the following verses and see whether you can find three ways that the moon can "declare the glory of God."

"And God said, Let there be lights in the firmament of the heaven to divide the day from the night; and let them be for signs, and for seasons, and for days, and years: And let them be for lights in the firmament of the heaven to give light upon the earth: and it was so." *Genesis 1:14-15*

Do you see that God made the moon and all "lights in the firmament" to be for signs, for seasons, and for lights in the heaven?

Relative sizes of moons to the planets they orbit

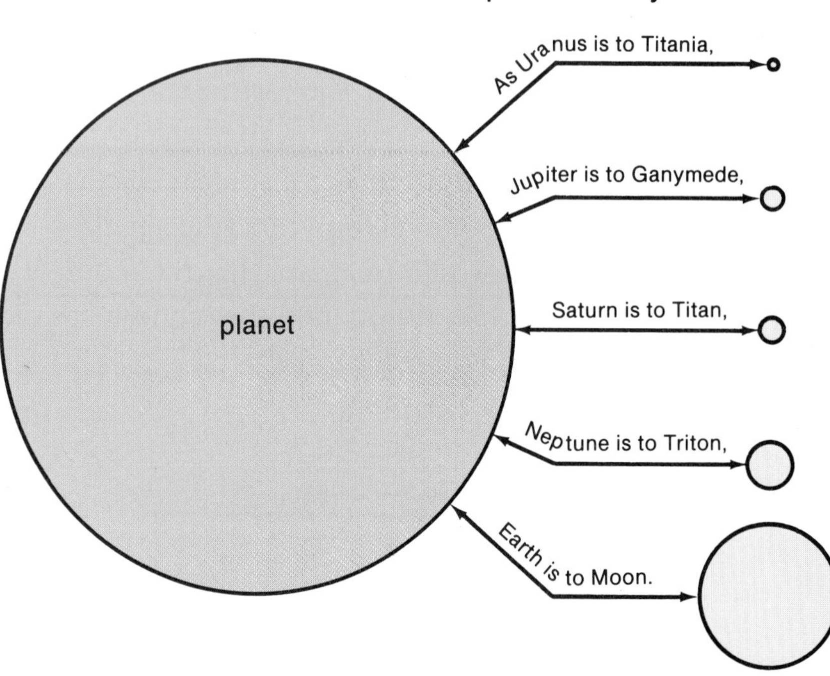

The Moon Is a Light

Although the moon does not make its own light, it does reflect some of the sun's light. Look at the chart. Since the moon is large for the size of the earth, it can reflect more light to the earth than any other moons can to their planets. If the moon were just average in size, a moonlit night would be too dark for certain organisms.

The large dark areas on the side of the moon facing the earth do not reflect as much light as other areas. The far side of the moon does not have as many dark areas. What would happen if the moon moved so that we could see the other side? If that happened, we could see the more reflective side of the moon, and a moonlit night might be too bright for plants and animals that need some time without much light.

Finding Out . . .

About How the Moon Moves

1. You will need plastic tack, a globe, and a softball.
2. Put a piece of plastic tack on the globe to show the place where you live. Have a friend hold a softball about a foot from the globe to represent the moon. Have him move the ball slowly around the globe as you turn it fast. Turn both counterclockwise. This activity will give you an idea of how the earth turns in comparison to the moon.
3. Now tell your friend to hold the moon steady while you slowly turn earth. Put the moon to the east of the U.S. Turn the globe half way around. Where is the moon in relation to the U.S. now? Is it in the west or the east? The rotation of the earth causes the moon to appear to move across the sky.

The Moon Is a Calendar

In the ancient Near East the moon was an important time measure. The people used each appearance of the new moon to start a "month." A merchant, for example, would take out his account book to find out how much people owed him. The Latin word for account book is *calends;* from it we get the word *calendar.* But later, people found it easier to divide the year into twelve parts. Each part had about the same number of days. So today the word "month" applies to the twelve sections of the year and has no connection with the appearance of a new moon.

The Moon Will Be a Warning

In Luke 21:25 Christ speaks of the end times. "There shall be signs in the sun, and in the moon, and in the stars; and upon the earth distress of nations, with perplexity." And Revelation 6:12 and 8:12 say, "The sun became black as sackcloth of hair, and the moon became as blood. . . . and the third part of the sun was smitten, and the third part of the moon . . . so as the third part of them was darkened, and the day shone not for a third part of it, and the night likewise." These verses tell us that God will use special signs, such as the darkening of the sun and the moon, to signal the end of this age. And at the end of this age Christ will come "in a cloud with power and great glory."

The perfect design and function of the moon point to a Creator much greater than His Creation. Isaiah 40:25-26 says, "To whom then will ye liken me, or shall I be equal? saith the Holy One. Lift up your eyes on high, and behold who hath created these things, that bringeth out their host by number: he calleth them all by names by the greatness of his might, for that he is strong in power; not one faileth."

The End of the Moon

God promises that the moon will continue as long as the earth remains. But when we have the new heaven and the new earth, the moon's purpose will be over. Revelation 21: 23 tells about the light of the new Jerusalem: "And the city had no need of the sun, neither of the moon, to shine in it: for the glory of God did lighten it, and the Lamb is the light thereof."

Insects, Arachnids, and Myriapods

The Insects

Did you know there are over 800,000 different kinds of insects? And some scientists think there are at least 800,000 more that have not yet been studied!

Yet despite their great numbers, they all have several characteristics in common. They all have exoskeletons made of *chitin.* They all have jointed *appendages,* or legs, that are paired equally. These characteristics make them *arthropods.* But they also have characteristics that make them *insects.*

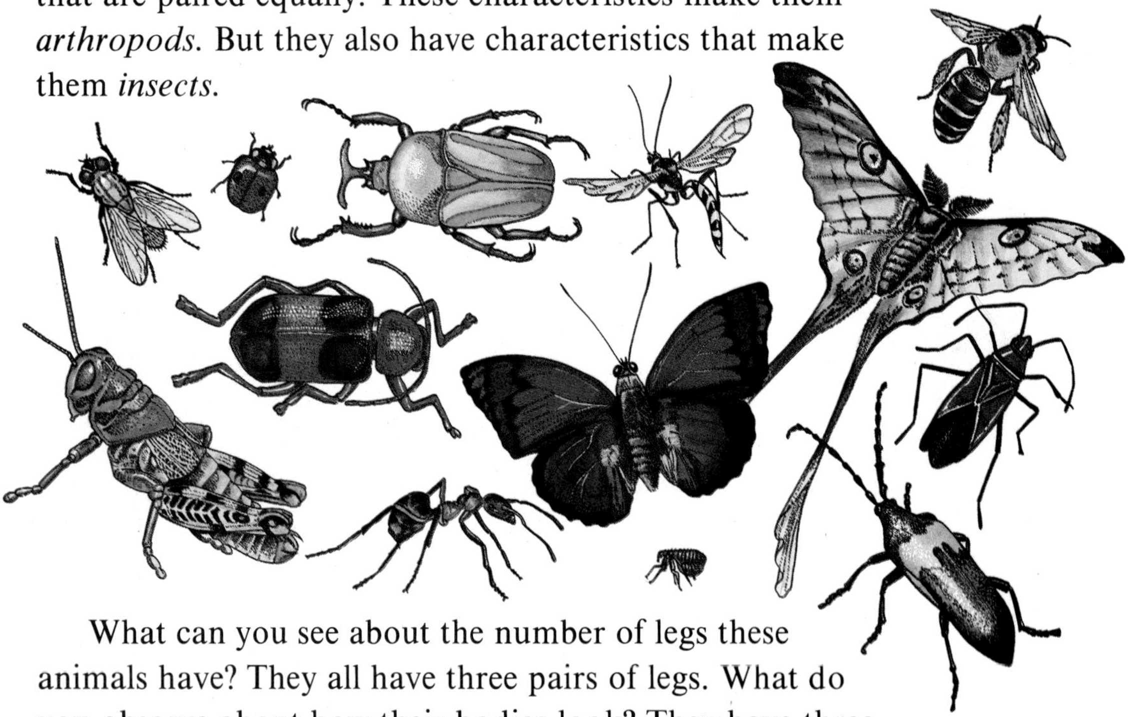

What can you see about the number of legs these animals have? They all have three pairs of legs. What do you observe about how their bodies look? They have three body segments, or divisions: the *head,* the *thorax,* and the *abdomen.* Can you make a generalization about their heads? Most have one pair of antennae on their heads.

What three characteristics can you say insects have? Insects also have characteristics that make them distinct from one another. Scientists use such characteristics to divide insects into smaller groups. Why do you think that scientists make these divisions?

The Grasshopper Group

The grasshopper, the praying mantis, the cricket, and the walking stick are members of the same group, or *order*. These insects have jaws that chew from side to side. They mostly chew up plants.

The praying mantis, however, eats other insects—even other praying mantises. Can you see in this picture how the praying mantis got its name?

All insects in this group have two pairs of wings, one pair like heavy paper and the other pair like crisp, clear silk. Both pairs fold up, the thin pair closing under the heavy pair.

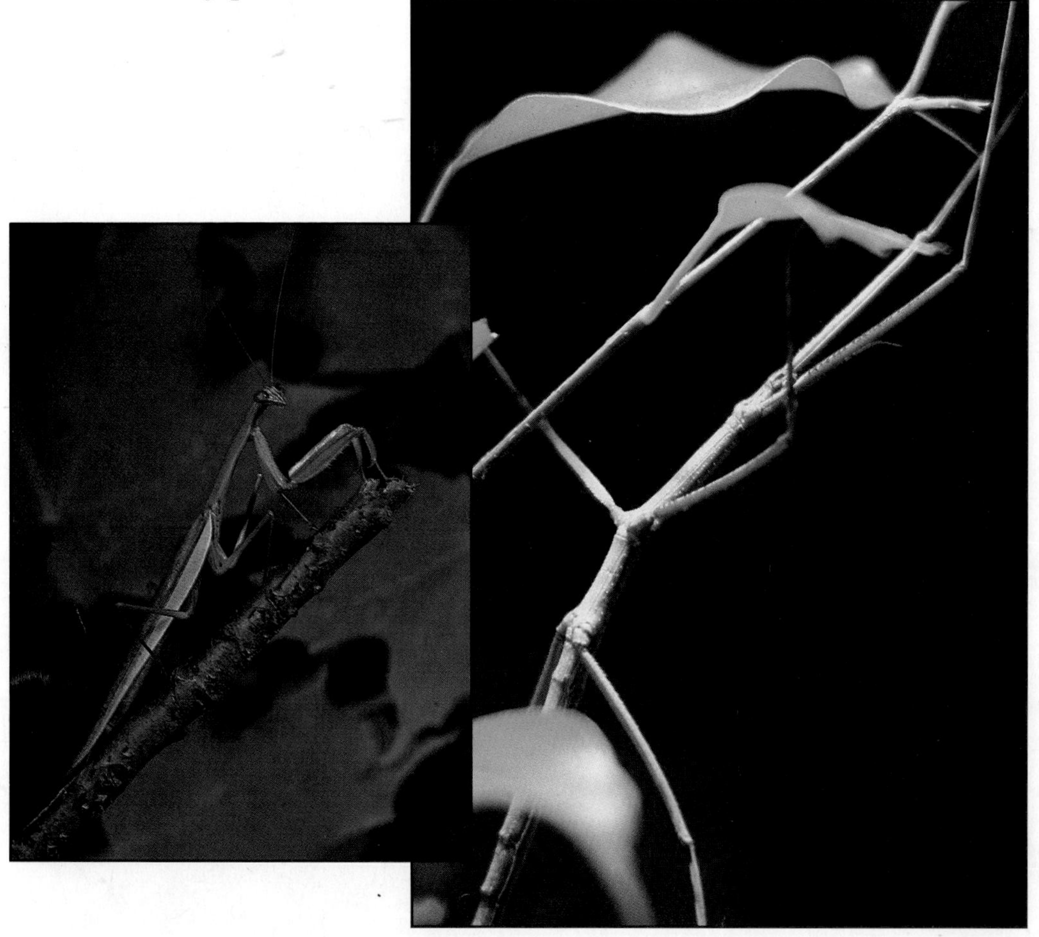

Young grasshoppers must go through a change to look like their parents. This change is called *metamorphosis.* Metamorphosis comes from the words *meta* and *morphi,* which means "form." What do you think *meta* means?

Many invertebrates also go through metamorphosis. Some, like the grasshopper, go through *incomplete metamorphosis.*

The grasshopper starts out as an *egg.* It then becomes a *nymph.* The nymph looks like the adult but is smaller and has no wings. Then it finally becomes an *adult* grasshopper. How many steps are there in incomplete metamorphosis?

The Dragonfly Group

The dragonfly and the damselfly are members of this group. They both have thin bodies shaped like darning needles. Dragonflies can be up to three inches long; damselflies are somewhat smaller.

They both have two pairs of wings, like veined cellophane. The wings of dragonflies usually stick straight out from their bodies. The wings of damselflies are held together above the body.

These insects eat mosquitoes, gnats, praying mantises, and just about any other insect. They lay their eggs in water and on plants such as the water lily and the cattail. Where would be a good place to go if you wanted to see a dragonfly?

The Aphid Group

The insects in this group can look like tiny tents when they are sitting still. They fold their wings so that they touch at the upper edges and spread out over their bodies. Most insects in this group have two pairs of wings, but some have none at all. How do you think scientists tell an insect is an aphid if it has no wings?

All aphids suck the juices out of plants. Most of them do a great deal of damage to gardens and house plants. One member of the aphid group is useful, though. The lac insect gives a sticky liquid that is used to make shellac, a thin varnish for wood.

Another member, the cicada, or seventeen-year locust, lays its eggs in trees. When the young hatch, they crawl to the ground and burrow into the soil. The nymphs live there on the juices from the plant roots. After seventeen years, they climb back up the tree and become adult cicadas.

The Bug Group

What is a bug? Many people call any insect or even a spider or a centipede a bug. Some people with the flu say they have "come down with a bug." Police detectives find a listening device on a telephone and report, "This phone has a bug." If a machine does not work right, the mechanic might explain: "I don't have all the bugs out yet."

But when scientists say *bugs,* they mean a special group of insects that have long, piercing mouth parts, almost like thin, miniature beaks. Most bugs have flat, oval bodies and two pairs of wings. Both pairs of wings are thin, but the front wings are thicker where they join the body and gradually get thinner. A few bugs do not have wings. How do we know they are bugs?

Some common bugs are stinkbugs, bedbugs, and water striders. Water striders can walk on the surface of ponds and streams.

The giant water bug lives in lakes and ponds. Some get up to four inches long and eat snails, minnows, and even small snakes. It has strong forelegs and a nasty bite.

Where do you think bedbugs live? How do you think stinkbugs got their name? How do you think the expression "Don't bug me" came about?

The Moth and Butterfly Group

At first glance, moths and butterflies look much alike. But take a close look at the butterfly and the moth pictured here. Can you find two ways moths are different from butterflies? How is a butterfly's body different from a moth's? How are the moth's antennae different from a butterfly's?

Moths and butterflies have large, delicate, and often colorful wings that are covered with tiny scales. Most moths do not have all the beautiful colors on their wings that butterflies do.

Most moths and all butterflies have long tube-like mouths that can reach deep into flowers for *nectar,* a sweet liquid. When not in use, the tube is coiled up under the head.

Monarch butterflies live in the northern United States during the summer. In early fall they gather in large groups and fly to the Gulf and Pacific coasts. When they land, they look like great orange clouds billowing down on the trees. In the spring, they fly north again.

Monarchs go through *complete metamorphosis.* Complete metamorphosis begins with an *egg.* The *larva* hatches from the egg. The larva then goes into the *pupa* stage, or resting period. The pupa builds a *chrysalis* and becomes encased in it. After a while, an adult monarch emerges from the chrysalis.

Some butterflies and many moths are harmful. The larvae, or caterpillars, eat fruits, vegetables, tree leaves, and even cotton or wool. The gypsy moth, for example, can destroy whole forests, stripping the leaves from trees. However, most of these insects do help pollinate flowers, and the silkworm moth gives us what we need to make silk cloth.

Butterflies

1. Thin bodies
2. Slender antennae
3. Rest with wings straight up
4. Fly mostly during the day
5. Develop from a chrysalis

Moths

1. Fat bodies
2. Feathery antennae
3. Rest with wings straight out
4. Fly mostly at night
5. Develop from a cocoon

The Beetle Group

There are at least 300,000 kinds of beetles. Some of them are known by the name *beetle,* but many of them are not. The Japanese beetle, the boll weevil, and the ladybug (ladybird beetle) belong to this group.

Beetles have two pairs of wings. The front wings are hard and usually shiny. When folded back, these wings make a shell-like covering with a straight line down the back.

Many of these insects eat plants, such as potato plants, wheat, and cotton, that are useful to people. A few however, like the ladybug, eat other insects.

If you find a ladybug, what should you do?

The Fly and Mosquito Group

Who hasn't had a housefly pester him at a meal, and who hasn't felt a mosquito helping itself to a little blood? The insects in this group are some of the least useful and most disliked insects around.

All members of this group have one pair of wings: thin, almost transparent, and veined. Most have sucking mouth parts. Deer flies and tsetse flies, for example—and, certainly, mosquitoes—do. Houseflies have sponging mouth parts.

Because flies lay their eggs in manure and walk in dirty places, they pick up bacteria on their claws and mouth parts and on the sticky hairs of their legs.

The claws, pads, and sticky hairs help them walk almost anywhere—even on glass. When the fly lands on someone's food, it can spread disease by rubbing some bacteria from its feet or mouth parts onto the food.

The mosquito likes to feed on animal and human blood. It spreads disease when it bites a sick animal or human and then flies off to bite another, leaving some diseased blood in its next victim.

Mosquitoes carry malaria from person to person. This disease was once thought to be brought on by bad air. Can you see how malaria got its name: *mal-* (bad) + *aria* (air)?

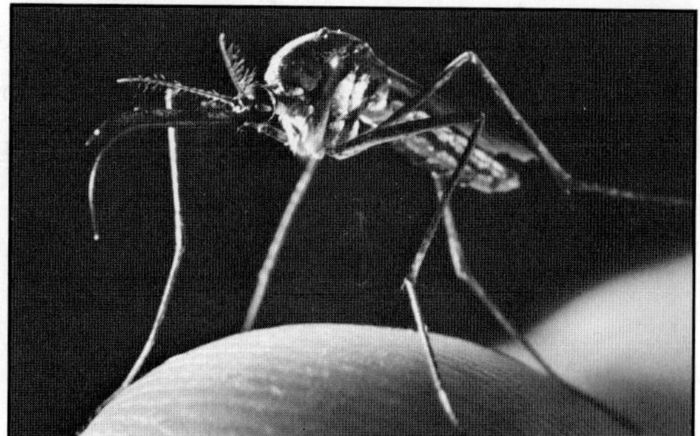

The Bee and Ant Group

Nearly everyone has dodged a bee or two, and many have felt the burning sting when the dodge is not fast enough.

Only female bees have stingers. But all bees have two pairs of wings, the front wings being much larger than the back. The thorax and the abdomen of all bees are distinctly divided, sometimes seeming to be joined by a mere thread.

Bees are a well-organized group. They are hard working, consistent, and efficient. Every bee has a job to do in the *colony,* or community—and it does it. The *queen bee* lays eggs, making sure that the colony always has enough workers. The *worker bees* build the hive, make the honey, and take care of the eggs. The *drones* are male bees that mate with the queen.

The worker bees have many skills. They are wonderful builders. They not only make their own building materials but also produce one of the neatest, most efficient structures in nature. To store honey and protect the eggs, workers form thousands of six-sided cells out of wax. This wax comes out of the workers' abdomens, usually after the bees have eaten a lot of honey.

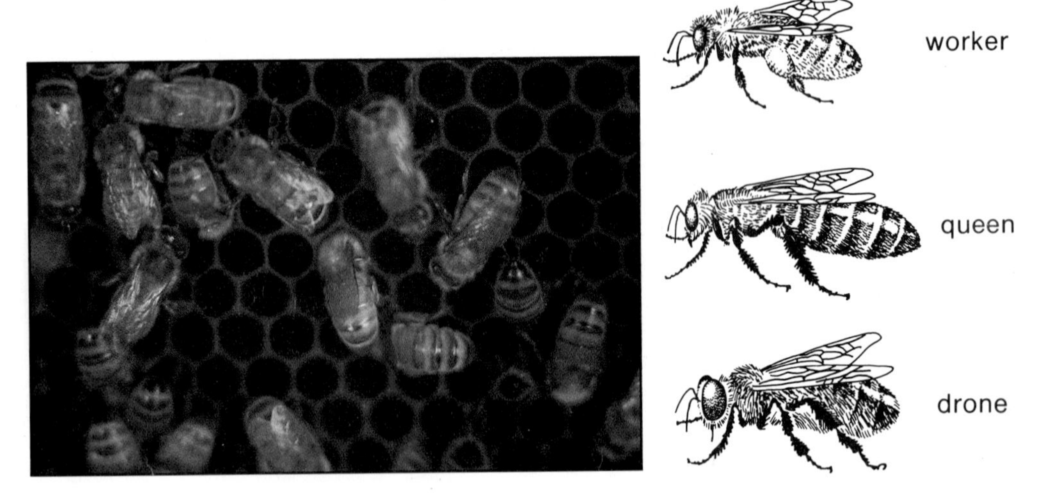

The six-sided cells in a bee hive are so regular in size that the width of a cell was once suggested as an international unit of measure. The six-sided shape makes the best possible use of space and is the strongest form the bees could use to support the hive.

The workers are also good harvesters. They gather pollen and nectar and carry it back to the hive in little pockets on each back leg called *pollen baskets.*

Bees can be good communicators. When a bee finds a rich source of pollen or nectar, it returns to the hive and does a little "dance," which actually forms a miniature map. The other bees learn "the map," which takes into account not only direction but also time of day and distance.

Perhaps most important to us, the workers are efficient sweet-makers. Bees make honey from the nectar they collect. At first the sweet liquid is runny, but the bees fan it with their wings to make extra water evaporate. Then the honey thickens. Where do you think we got the phrase "busy as a bee"?

Finding Out . . .

About Ants

1. Get a large, wide-mouthed jar; an unopened can (large enough to leave one and one-half inches between it and the sides of the jar); some soil; bread crumbs, jelly, or sugar; a small sponge; a swatch of loosely woven cloth; black construction paper; a large rubber band; and some ants.
2. Put the sealed can inside the jar and fill the space left with soil to within one inch of the top. Place the food and the sponge dampened with water on top of the soil. Put in the ants. Cover the jar with the loosely woven cloth and secure with a rubber band.
3. When not observing the ants, cover the outside of the jar with black construction paper. Try giving the ants different kinds of foods. Record your observations over a period of a week.

Another hard-working insect is the ant. Even the Bible commends their industry. Ants look something like bees, although rarely do any but queen ants and the males have wings. The ants have distinct body segments: head, thorax, and abdomen. Many ants have no "stingers," but their powerful jaws can deliver a bite that may feel like a sting.

Like bees, ants divide up the work in their colonies. The leafcutter ants, for example, have jobs according to the size of the worker. The largest leafcutter ant is the queen. Her job is to dig the first tunnel, lay the eggs, and begin a colony. Next in size are the soldier ants, big-headed, sharp-jawed insects that can kill enemy insects ten times their size. They guard the queen and the colony. Smaller ants, the workers, give the whole group its name; they are the ones that actually cut leaves. This group goes out into an Amazon forest in long lines sometimes twelve-ants wide. They cut up leaves and carry the pieces home. From a distance these streams of ants, going and coming between forest and nest, look like little conveyor belts in a very busy factory.

To do the same amount of work as a leafcutter, a man would have to run ten miles in forty minutes—carrying an 800-pound weight over his head. And he would have to do that at least seven times a day.

Back at the colony, smaller ants carry the pieces of leaf down the many tunnels and give them to the smallest ants of all. These tiny insects—about the size of an eye in a regular sewing needle—chew up the leaves and use them to grow a fungus. All the ants in the colony eat this fungus and nothing else. Since a colony can contain as many as four million ants, it is important that each ant do its job in this process of growing food.

Some ants are like little dairy farmers. They keep and feed their "cows," the aphids. When stroked by the ants' feelers, the aphids give a sweet liquid. The ants need this "milk" and seem to do "chores" to get it.

"Go to the ant, thou sluggard; consider her ways, and be wise: Which having no guide, overseer, or ruler, Provideth her meat in the summer, and gathereth her food in the harvest." *Proverbs 6:6-8*

The Flea Group

The fleas have a group name, *Siphonaptera,* that means "siphon without wings." What can you guess about the flea's mouth? What can you guess about how the flea gets around?

Fleas have sucking tubes for eating and legs designed for leaping. One kind of flea can jump thirteen inches in one jump. You probably think fleas are the pests on dogs. But fleas feast on many hosts, including people. And they hop from one host to another at any opportunity.

Although the flea is a small animal, it has carried death to millions. In the 900s, fleas from sick rats spread a plague known as the Black Death throughout Asia and Europe. The plague wiped out one-fourth of the population of Europe. In the late 1800s, another pandemic began when ships from Hong Kong traveled to many ports around the world with diseased rats aboard. In India alone, 10,000,000 people died within twenty years.

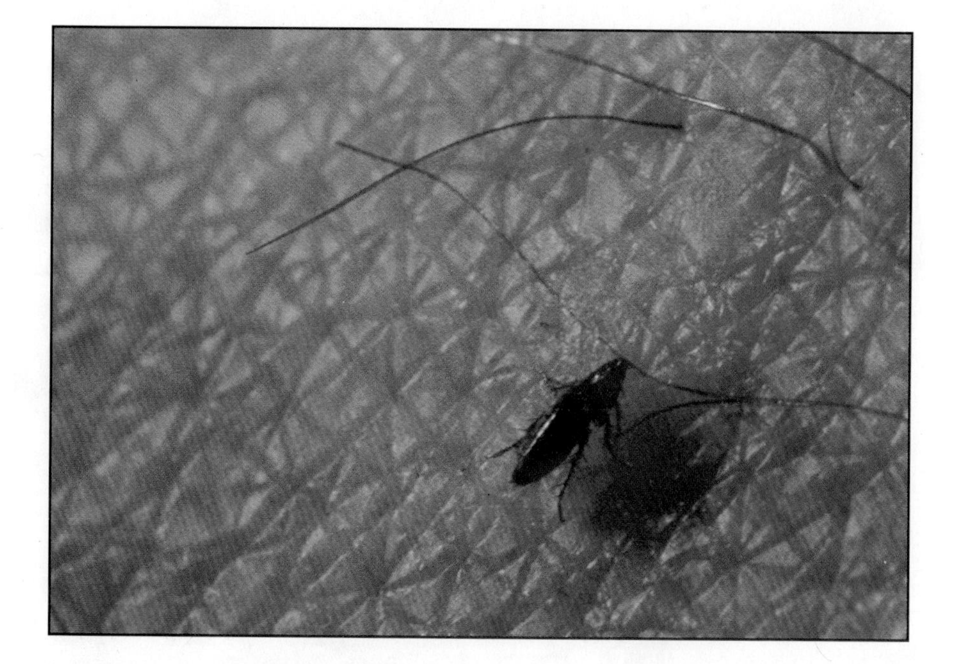

Finding Out . . .

About Insects

1. Get a plastic margarine container with a lid and five sealable sandwich bags.
2. Catch an insect in the container and then put it into a sandwich bag. Without crushing the insect, try to keep its wings spread. Catch and seal at least five insects this way. Try to get insects that look as different from each other as possible.
3. Put the bags into the freezer for an hour.
4. Bring your insects to class in the bags. With your teacher's help, classify and mount your insects.
5. Display your mounted insects with those of your classmates.

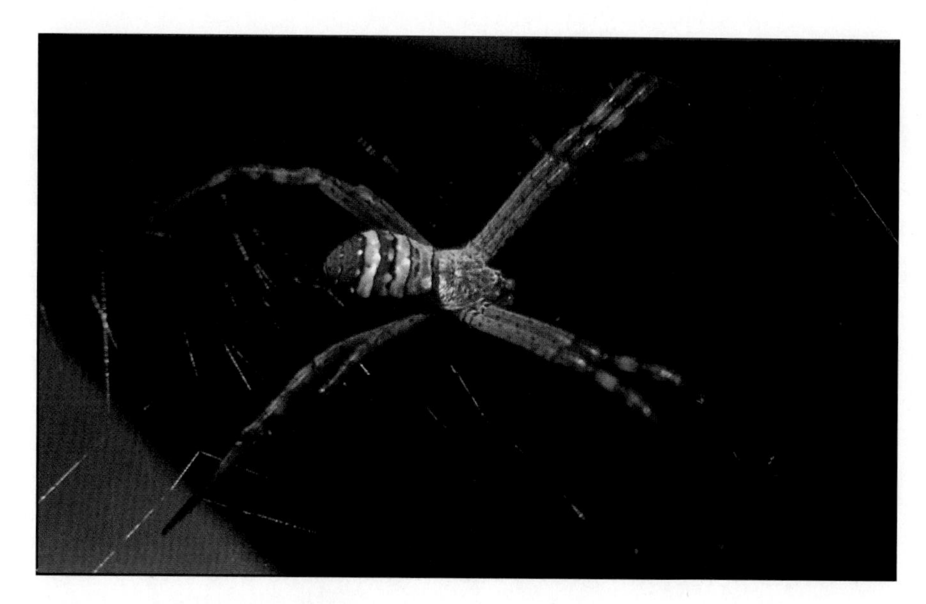

The Arachnids

The ancient Greeks had a story about a beautiful girl who could weave better than anyone else. One day she challenged the goddess Athena to a weaving contest. Athena was outraged that a mere mortal would claim to be as good a weaver as she. In anger, she changed the girl into a spider. The girl's name was Arachne, and her name became the name for arthropods in the spider class—*arachnids.* Why do you think spiders were named after her?

Spiders, scorpions, daddy longlegs, and ticks all have common characteristics. Like all arthropods they have an exoskeleton and jointed appendages. But they also have qualities that make them distinct from other arthropods.

How does a spider look different from an ant? Arachnids have four pairs of legs. The head and thorax of a spider are joined, seeming to be one part. How is the ant different in structure? Why is a spider not an insect?

Arachnids do not have antennae. Spiders do, however, have two pairs of appendages on their heads, for poisoning and holding their victims. Do arachnids have wings?

Spiders are the most misunderstood of arthropods. Killed on sight many times, they are actually helpful to man. They feed mostly on insects, controlling pests.

Spiders get their food in many different ways. Many, of course, build webs. Although one strand of a cobweb may look fragile, it is surprisingly strong. A web needs to be strong—it is the spider's home. Very large insects that get caught in a sticky web cannot usually struggle free. Even hummingbirds have gotten tangled fast in the sturdy snares of spiders' webs. One study showed that if you could make a rope of web one inch thick it could hold up seventy tons!

Other spiders, however, use other tricks and traps. The trapdoor spider digs a hole in the ground and builds a door over it. The spider lurks under the partially open door. When an insect goes too near the door, the spider lunges out and grabs it.

Another kind of spider sometimes goes fishing. It perches on a plant near a stream or pond, occasionally dangling a leg in the water to attract fish. If a fish comes up, the spider waits until it is near the surface and then—jumps on it. Sinking his fang-like pinchers into it, the spider drags his catch ashore to eat it.

Two kinds of poisonous spiders are the brown recluse and the black widow. The brown recluse always has a violin-shaped yellow spot on its back. The black widow has yellow to red splotches that sometimes resemble an hourglass on the underside of its abdomen. Both spiders can inflict painful bites that cause vomiting, fever, muscle cramps, and sometimes death.

The scorpion has legs like a spider, but it also has a long, narrow abdomen that has pinchers and a stinger at the end. The stinger puts poison into the spiders and insects that the scorpion catches. If it stings a human, the scorpion can cause a painful swelling—but it rarely can kill. Can you find scorpions mentioned in the Bible?

The daddy longlegs looks like a tall, spindly spider. It eats insects such as plant lice. Who should especially like the daddy longlegs?

The Myriapods

The word *myriad* means "many"; *pod* means "foot." What do you think the name *myriapod* tells about the members of this group?

Centipedes and millipedes are myriapods. These are long, thin creatures with many body segments. *Centum* means "hundred" and *mille* means "thousand." *Pede* and *pod* come from the same word. Which myriapod has more legs?

Electricity

Electricity is a mystery. No one has ever observed it or heard it or felt it. We can see and hear and feel only what electricity *does.* We know that it makes light bulbs shine and irons heat up and telephones ring. But we cannot say what electricity itself is like.

We cannot even say where electricity comes from. Some scientists think that the sun may be the source of most electricity. Others think that the movement of the earth produces some of it. All anyone knows is that electricity seems to be everywhere and that there are many ways to bring it forth.

How would you have to change the way you get ready for school if you did not use electricity?

"The voice of thy thunder was in the heaven: the lightnings lightened the world: the earth trembled and shook."

Psalm 77:18

Static Electricity

Have you ever gotten a shock from a doorknob or someone's hand or your pet cat? You may know that the shock is *static electricity.* But did you know that the snap and spark of that encounter is—on a small, small scale—like the crash and flash of thunder and lightning in a storm?

The shock, the thunder, and the lightning all happen because static electricity "jumps" from one place to another place. The jump is caused by activity in the smallest realm we know of—the atom.

Atoms have three parts. In the center are *protons* and *neutrons.* Whirling around that center are *electrons.* An atom has as many electrons as it has protons. It is in balance; that is, it is *electrically neutral.* To make electricity act, the number of electrons and protons must be unbalanced.

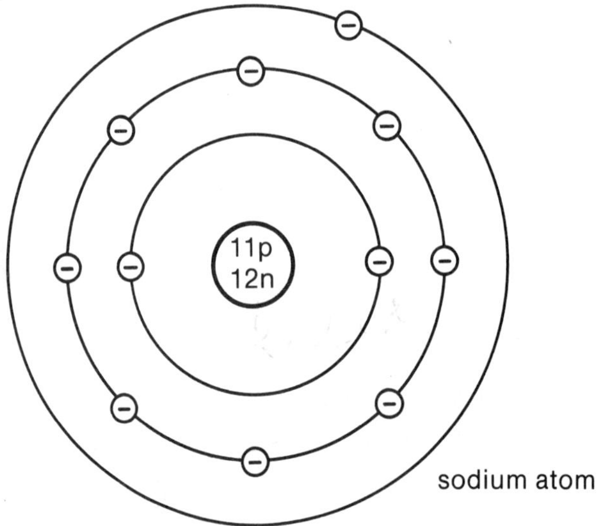

sodium atom

The oldest method of making electricity is to rub two objects together. The ancient Greeks found that *amber,* a stone of petrified sap, sparked when it was rubbed with fur. Their word for amber was *elektron.* How is our word *electricity* like that word?

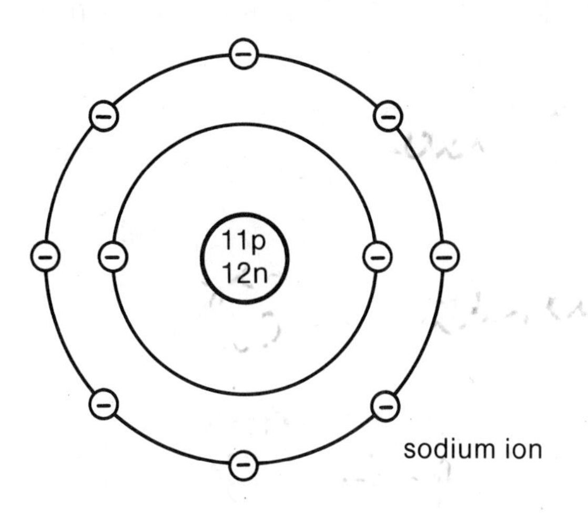

When two objects rub together, some of the electrons from one go over to the other. The balance of electrons in both objects is now disrupted. The objects are *charged.* If an object has more electrons than protons, it has a *minus charge.* If it has fewer electrons than protons, it has a *plus charge.*

When you walk across a carpet, your body gathers extra electrons. Do you have a minus charge or a plus charge? When you touch a metal knob, the electrons "jump" from your hand to the knob. You feel a sting and hear a snap. The electricity is then, we say, *grounded.*

Lightning flares in the sky for the same reason. Drops of water rub against the air in the clouds. Large drops—always plus-charged—fall toward the bottom of the clouds. The smaller, minus-charged drops stay higher in the clouds. For a while, the air keeps the different charges apart, or *insulates* them. But when it no longer can, the electricity jumps across the cloud or between clouds in a giant spark: lightning. We call the sound of that exchange *thunder.*

Sometimes the spark goes between the cloud and the earth. Why are tall buildings or the highest points in flat areas most likely to be hit?

Do you know a way that people try to make lightning travel into the earth, that is, to be grounded? They put lightning rods on tops of buildings. A heavy wire runs from the rod down the side of the building and onto a metal plate in the ground. If lightning strikes the rod, the wire carries the electricity into the ground.

Sometimes at night, sailors in tall ships see a dim glow wavering at the tops of the masts and at the ends of poles that hold the sails. Before sailors understood that the light was caused by static electricity passing from the ship into the air, they called it *St. Elmo's fire.* Imagine how strange it must have seemed to men who knew nothing of electricity to see the top of their masts glowing in the dark, but never burning or smoking.

Thunder and lightning and St. Elmo's fire all result from the action of static electricity. Why do you think St. Elmo's fire is a quiet glow and a thunderstorm has noisy flashes?

When you comb your hair on a dry, cold day, you probably notice that your hair follows the comb or brush. Sometimes your hair may even make a crackling sound. What you have done is bring out a little electricity by rubbing one thing—your hair—with another—the comb.

Another name for static electricity is *frictional electricity*. Can you tell why?

Your hairs follow the comb for the same reason that the Greeks' amber drew feathers or bits of straw. Objects that have different charges attract each other. Why do you think then that each strand of hair pushes away or *repels* every other strand of hair? Objects that have the same charge repel each other.

Finding Out . . .

About Static Electricity

1. Get two balloons, some string, and a wool sweater or gloves.
2. Blow up the balloons and tie each with a length of string. Rub one of the balloons several times on the sweater or with the gloves.
3. Hold the other balloon by the string and bring it near the balloon you just rubbed. What happens?
4. Now rub the other balloon with the wool. Holding both balloons by the strings, bring them close together. What happens?
5. Record your observations.

Current Electricity

Static comes from a word meaning "standing." Although static electricity sometimes jumps from one place to another, it does not keep moving. It is not very useful to us because it produces power only for a moment.

To be most useful, electricity must be moving. An electric current is a flow of moving charges. When electricity moves, it can do work for us.

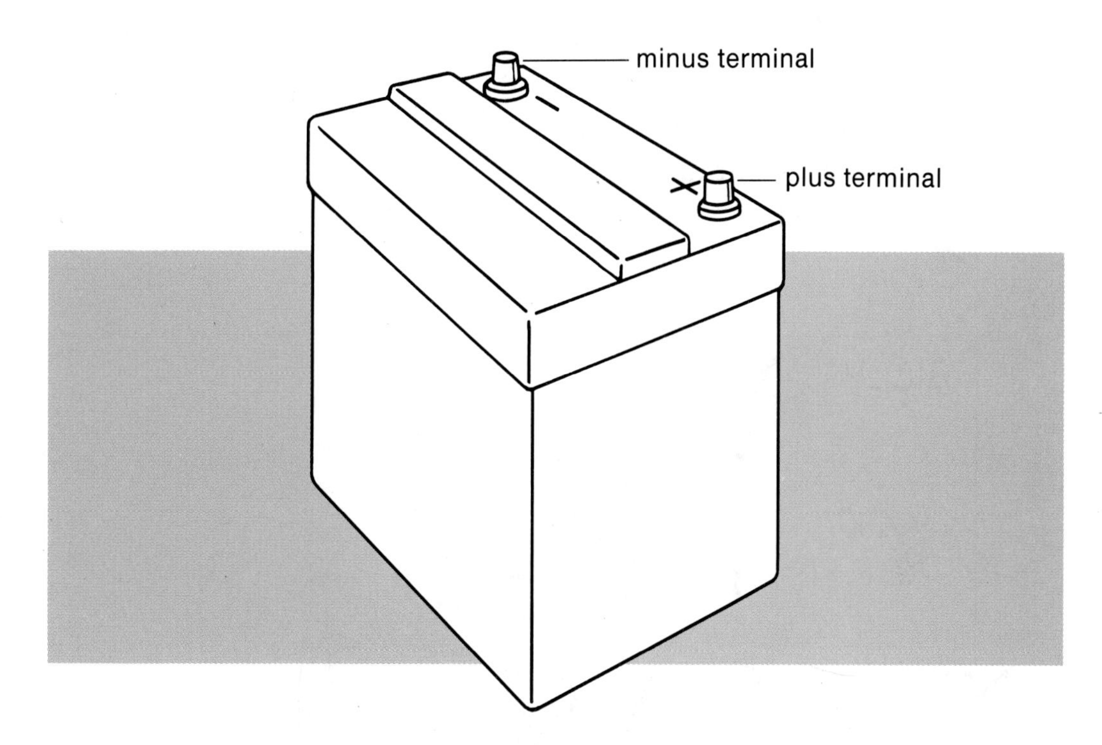

To keep electricity acting, you must keep electrons out of balance with the protons. One way to do that is to use chemicals. Some chemical actions will make electrons move from one place to another.

Can you think of some things that use *batteries?* A car does. The battery of a car contains chemicals that act together to take electrons away from one place on the battery called a *terminal.* Do you think that this terminal is a *plus* or a *minus* terminal? The battery also has another terminal. What do you think it is called?

The extra electrons from the terminal can travel if they have something to travel along. Suppose a wire that allows electrons to travel through it is hooked to the terminal. Where will the electrons go? They will go out through the wire. If the other end of the wire is hooked to the other terminal, where will the electrons go?

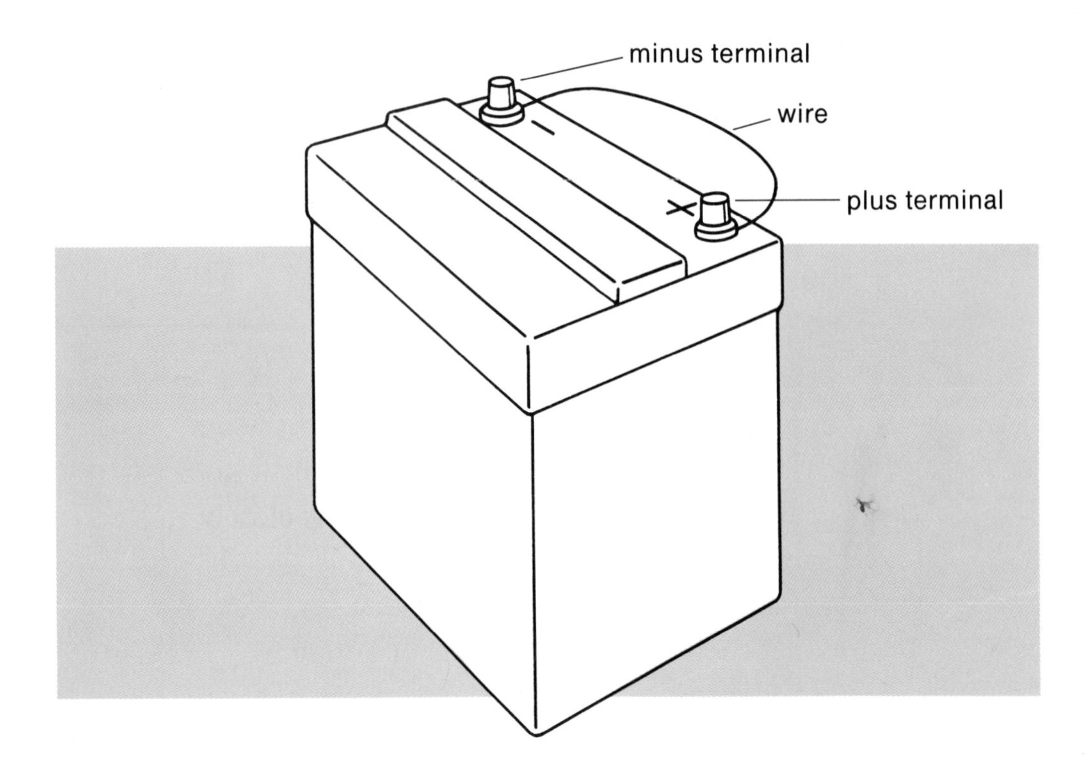

Out-of-balance electrons tend to get back in balance. At the second terminal, the electrons again get into the groups they were in before the chemicals acted. But the chemicals are still active; the electrons are freed again; they go to the terminal, out through the wire, and to the other terminal. Can you see how a battery keeps electricity moving?

To have current electricity, you need two things. You need something that will keep electrons out of balance as a battery does. And you need a complete circle or path—a *circuit.*

Circuit comes from a Latin word meaning "to go around." How is that name appropriate? What do you think a *circuit breaker* does?

Another way to keep electricity moving is to use a *generator.* A generator does not use chemicals. Why would it be better to find a way to make electricity without chemicals? Chemicals get old; they are used up; they are expensive.

Generate means "to make." But can a generator really "make" electricity? A generator actually gathers electricity and sends it where we can use it. Most generators change the force of magnetism into electricity.

Magnets can create a force. If you put two bar magnets together north end to south end, the magnets will pull together. If you put them together at like ends, they will push apart. The force that magnets make is closely related to electricity.

When a magnet is moved over metal, a current is produced. When metal is moved over a magnet, a current is produced. What has to happen for the current to be constantly produced? Either the magnet or the metal has to keep moving.

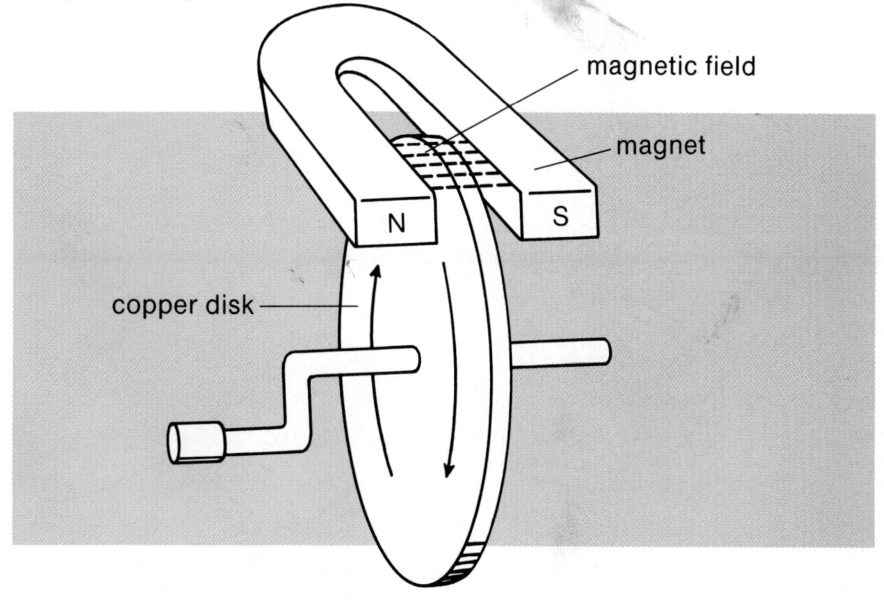

You can produce a current by moving a magnet over a metal wire that is part of a circuit. Do you think you could send enough electricity along a wire this way to light an electric bulb? Do you think, if you could, that you would be able to keep it lit long? You would probably soon decide that you would rather sit in the dark than try to keep the electricity coming.

In 1831 a man named Michael Faraday had come to about the same conclusion. He had tried a dozen ways to increase the power of his magnet and wire current-maker. He even carried a magnet and wire around in his pocket to help him think about the problem. One day, as he worked in his laboratory, he happened to wrap a wire around a ring several times. He looked at the coil in his hand, and suddenly, after months of pondering, he had an idea.

Faraday made another coil of wire and hooked the wire ends to a meter that registered electrical current. When he passed a magnet in and out of the coil, a *solenoid,* the needle on the meter shot over to the right. He had generated electricity!

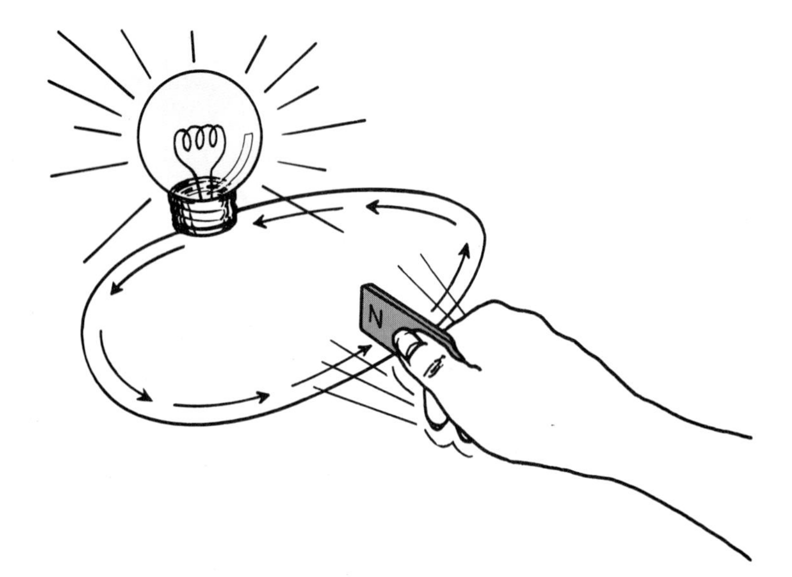

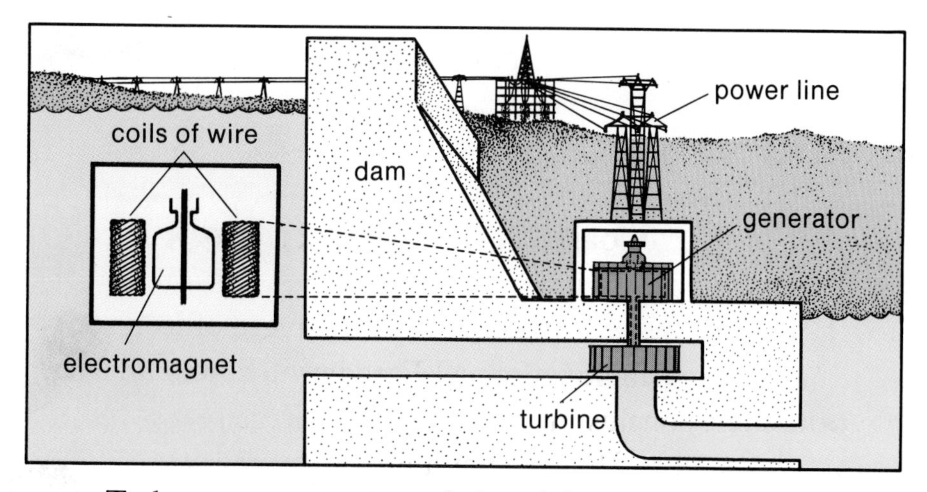

Today great amounts of electricity come from huge generators that work on the same basis. Giant coils, electromagnets called *field coils,* produce thousands of times as much current as Faraday's first small experiment. Water is often used to turn the coils.

Big dams provide the water power for such generators. The water pours into the dam. The energy of the rushing water turns a water wheel called a *turbine.* The turbine causes the coils to turn; the turning coils produce an electrical current; the electricity travels out of the generators and is sent out to hundreds of houses and industries.

If you were to go on a tour to a big dam, an elevator would whisk you down into the middle of the dam. You would be about fifty stories below the top of the dam when you stepped out of the elevator. Then you would walk into the powerhouse, a huge room with long windows that look out over the river. In this room are the generators, which make only a quiet hum. But these generators are putting out more energy than fifty thousand wild horses.

Mr. Faraday would certainly be surprised to see the uses his invention has been put to. If he could visit your classroom, what would you show him first?

Finding Out . . .

About Electromagnets

1. Get one meter of insulated wire, a piece of iron rod, several small paper clips, a knife switch, and an energy source.

2. Following your teacher's instructions, wrap the wire around the iron rod. Then attach the iron and the wire to the knife switch and the energy source.

3. Find out whether your electromagnet will lift a paper clip. Will it lift two? Record your observations.

Plants

"Build ye houses, and dwell in them; and plant gardens, and eat the fruit of them." *Jeremiah 29:5*

God created many different plants. How are plants alike, and how are they different? How can you tell one plant from another plant? To decide, you need to look closely at the parts of a plant. For example, are there leaves? What shape are the leaves? What size? Are there flowers? What color are the flowers? How big are the flowers? Are the stems soft or woody?

Answering questions like these will help you to *classify* or "group" plants. Can you think of some things that are put into groups by how they are alike? How about books in libraries? All the history books are together, and all the science books are together. Why do we make groups of things like books?

Scientists classify plants to help identify them. Scientists who study plants are called *botanists.* Botanists look at the parts of plants and observe how plants are alike or different. Plants are classified into two large groups: those *with tubes* and those *without tubes.*

Do you remember what tubes carry? They carry food and water inside the leaves, stems, and roots. You can see such tubes if you break a stalk of celery in half.

Plants with No Tubes

Plants with no tubes usually grow close to water or in damp, shady places. Why do you think they grow there?

Fungi

Fungi are not green because they have no chlorophyll. Does a plant need chlorophyll to make food? How can a plant live without chlorophyll? Because fungi do not make their food, they do not need chlorophyll. If they do not make food, how do you suppose they get food? Fungi get their food from other organisms that may be dead or alive. Have you seen these fungi? Where are they getting their food?

Finding Out . . .

About Fungi

1. Get one old orange or cantaloupe, a magnifying glass, and a large glass jar.
2. Let the fruit sit out all day. Then cover it with the jar. Leave it for several days until mold appears.
3. Remove the jar and observe the mold under a magnifying glass. Record your observations.

These fungi are called *molds.* They grow on fruit, bread, and even bathtubs and showers. Another fungus is the mushroom. Mushrooms grow on soil and on living or dead trees. Have you seen these mushrooms?

Fungi produce other fungi by microscopic round structures called *spores.* The fungi produce so many spores that at times appear to be a cloud of smoke coming from the fungus.

People eat some kinds of mushrooms. You can buy them in grocery stores. Never eat a mushroom you find growing in your yard or in the woods. It may be a poisonous kind!

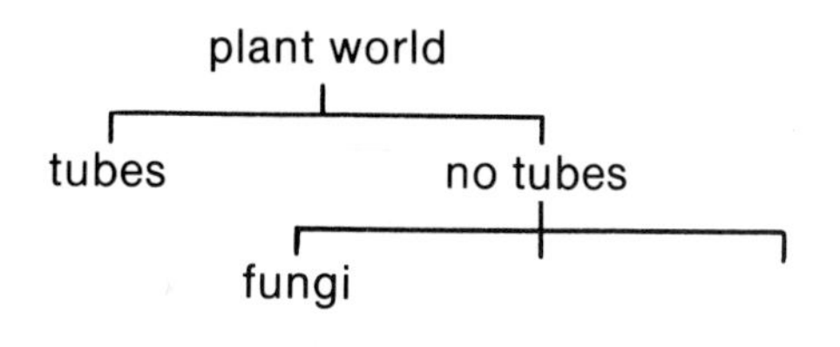

Algae

A second group of tubeless plants are the *algae. Algae* comes from a Latin word meaning "seaweed."

Algae are small or large. Some can be seen only through a microscope. Others may be as long as a football field. Algae are grouped by color. They may be green, bluish green, brown, or red. They all have chlorophyll. Do they make their own food?

Algae grow in ponds, streams, lakes, or oceans. The brown and red algae usually grow in the ocean. Most of the green and bluish green algae grow in ponds and streams.

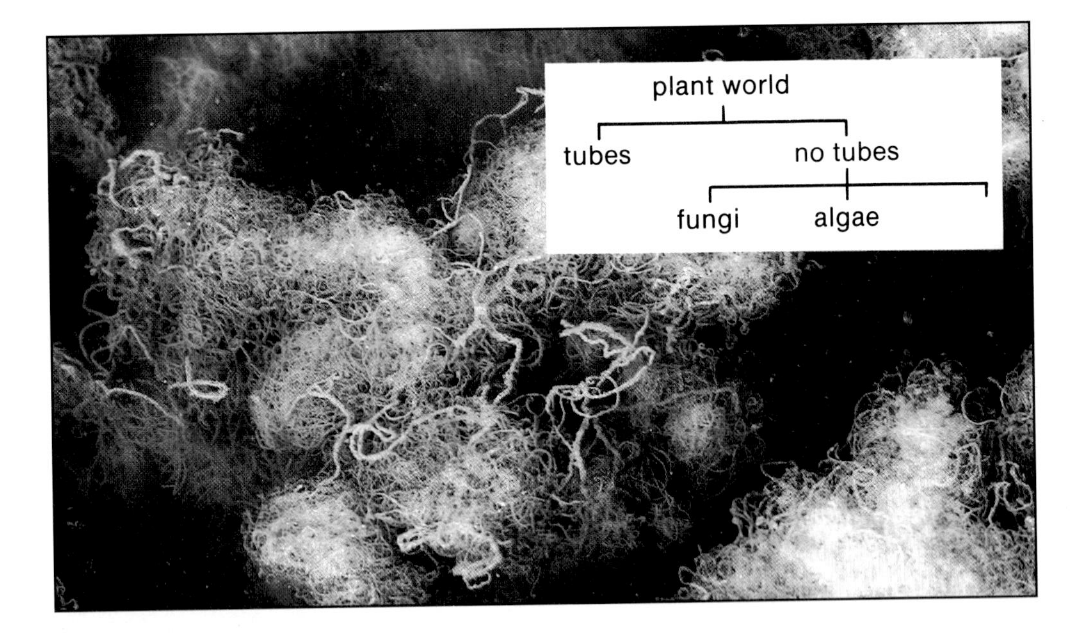

Algae may also live on land. For example, some grow on brick walks, and others grow on tree trunks. Most of these are green algae.

Many animals eat algae for food, and people use algae to make many products. For example, a material from brown algae is used in ice cream and whipped-cream products.

Mosses and Liverworts

These small green plants grow in damp, shady places—on rocks, on trees, and in soil. A few grow in the water.

Mosses and liverworts grow from spores. What other tubeless plant grows from spores? Special structures form at the top of plants which hold the spores. They are called *capsules*. When the capsule bursts open, the spores escape and are carried by the wind to new places to grow.

Mosses and liverworts grow in many places—from tropical jungles to arctic rocks. Sometimes the mosses and liverworts grow so close together that a soft, green carpet or cushion is formed over rocks and soil.

Plants with Tubes

Most of the plants God created have tubes. These plants all have roots, stems, and leaves. They are said to be "true" plants because they have tubes in them. Some of the mosses and liverworts have structures which *look like* roots, stems, and leaves. But remember, mosses and liverworts have *no* tubes.

Since there are so many kinds of plants with tubes, botanists have classified the tubed plants into two smaller groups: those that produce seeds and those that do not.

Plants with No Seeds

A group of tubed plants that do not produce seeds are the *ferns.* God created many different and beautiful ferns. Most ferns have large, split leaves called *fronds.* Look at the fronds on these ferns. Have you seen any of them before?

New fronds are all curled up, and as they grow they uncurl. The curled-up fronds are called *fiddleheads.* Can you guess why? In the northeastern United States people eat fiddleheads. You can buy them there in some grocery stores.

Ferns produce new ferns by spores. The spores are produced on the underside of their leaves. Have you ever seen rows of small brown lumps on ferns? Those lumps are not bugs but spore containers.

The small brown lumps will burst open, and the tiny spores will fall to the ground, or they will be carried away by the wind. If a spore lands where it is warm, moist, and shaded, the spore will become a new fern.

You can find ferns in many places in the world. They are most abundant in forests and in the tropics. Do you have any ferns growing around your house?

Plants with Seeds

Most plants with tubes produce seeds. Botanists classify the seed plants into two groups: those that produce seeds in flowers and fruits and those that produce seeds in cones.

Conifers

Conifers are cone-producing trees. Have you ever seen any of these conifers?

Conifer leaves have two basic shapes. Can you tell what those two shapes are by looking at these pictures?

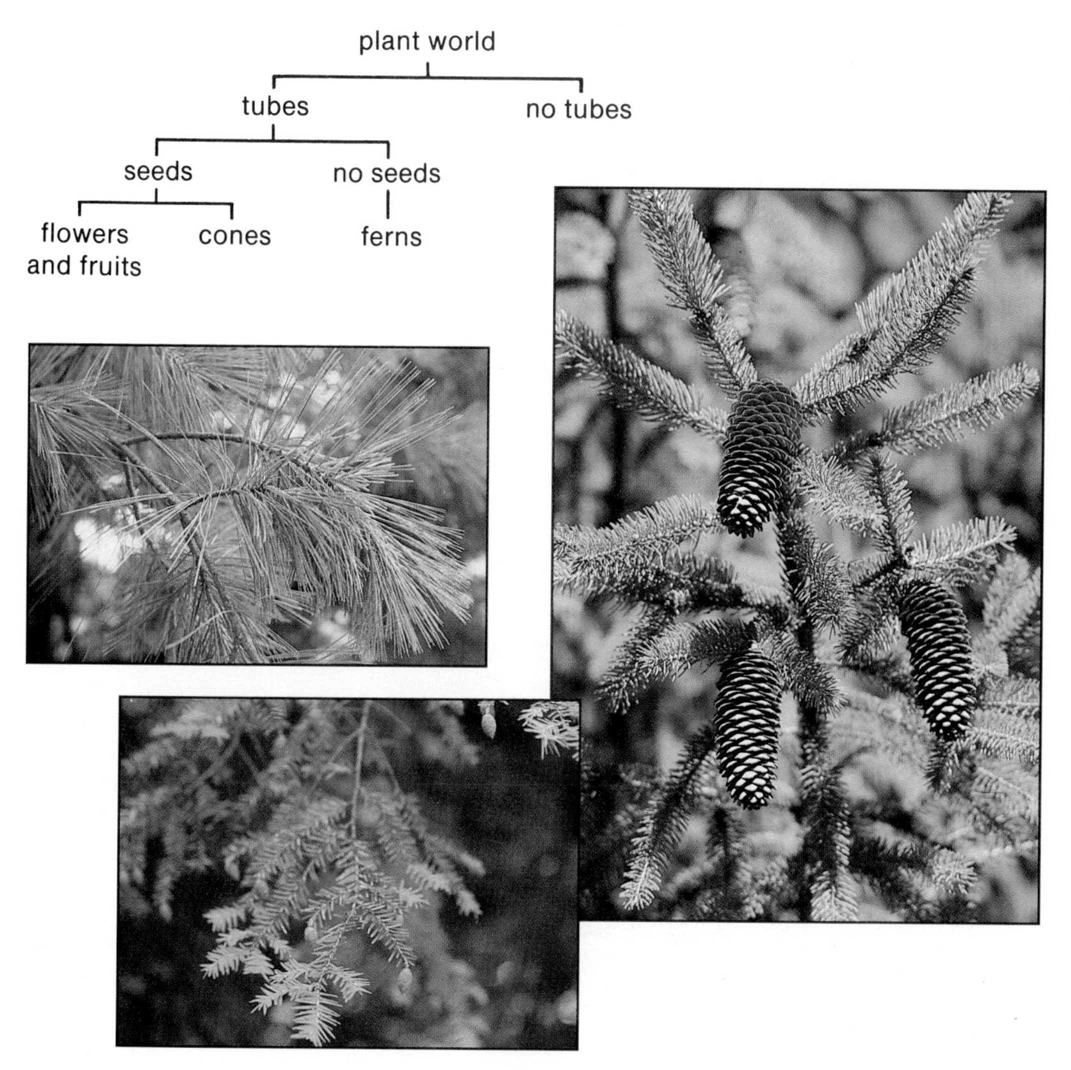

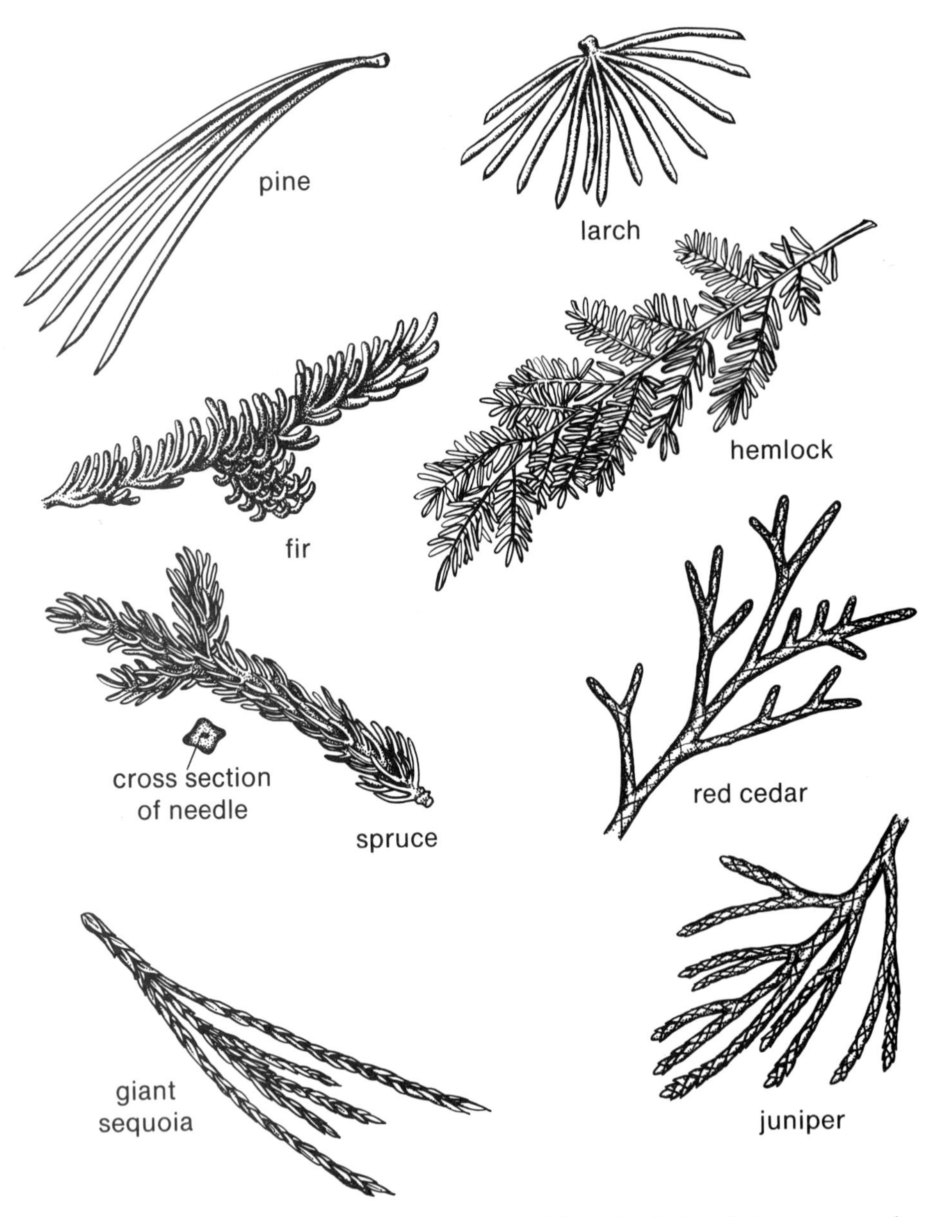

Conifers are sometimes grouped by their leaf shapes and sizes. Pines and larches, for example, have needlelike leaves in clusters.

Firs and hemlocks, on the other hand, have flattened needles. Hemlock needles are shorter than the fir needles.

Spruce needles have four sides. How can you tell a spruce needle from a hemlock needle?

Cedars, redwoods, and sequoias all have scalelike leaves. Look at the photographs. Try to name the conifers pictured below.

Because most conifers do not lose their leaves in the fall, they are said to be *evergreen.* A larch and a dawn redwood will lose their leaves every fall. Trees that lose their leaves are *deciduous.*

Finding Out . . .

About Conifers

1. Get some spruce needles, a small pair of scissors, and a magnifying glass.
2. Cut a needle in half crossways.
3. Look at the cut end straight on under the magnifying glass. Can you see the four sides?
4. You are looking at a *cross section* of a spruce needle.
5. Record how the cross section looks.

Conifer cones grow in many different shapes and sizes. Look at the picture. Have you ever seen any of these cones? Where have you seen them?

How would you describe each of these cones? Are they long and narrow? Big and fat? Short and narrow? Spiny? How are they different from each other?

Some conifers do not have cones like most of the other conifers. Their cones are berrylike. Junipers have this type of cone. The oil from juniper berries is used in making perfumes and medicines.

Because conifer wood is soft, we can make many products from it. Paper comes from the wood of conifers, and so does lumber for houses. Whole trunks of some conifers become telephone poles and boat docks. Can you think of any other things made from woods like pine and cedar?

Flower and Fruit-Producing Plants

Plants that make seeds in flowers and fruits are called *flowering plants*. There are some parts that all flowers have. You can see these parts in the drawing below.

The petals are usually the most colorful part of the flower. God has created many beautiful and colorful petals.

The male part of the flower is the *stamen*. At the top of the stamen are small *pollen sacs* containing the powdery grains of pollen. The female part of the flower is the *carpel*. The bottom of the carpel is the *ovary*. A fully developed ovary is a *fruit*. When you hear the word "fruit," what do you think of? Do you think of apples, bananas, or grapes? But did you know that tomatoes and corn are fruit? Cucumbers and squashes are fruits too.

Inside a fruit are seeds. Sometimes there is only one seed inside. Can you think of a fruit with only one seed inside? Name some fruits that have more than one seed inside. What will a seed become?

About half of all the plants in the world are flowering plants. Flowering plants can be large or small. Many trees have flowers. Can you name some trees that have flowers?

Grasses have flowers too. They are small and have no color. Perhaps you have seen grass flowers and did not know they were flowers at all.

Botanists have divided flowering plants into two classes: the *monocotyledons* and the *dicotyledons*.

Monocots are flowering plants whose first sprout has one leaf. This first structure is called a *seed leaf*. Dicots have two seed leaves. Seed leaves have food in them that feeds the tiny new plant.

The "cotyledon" part of the words *dicotyledon* and *monocotyledon* comes from a word that means "cup-shaped." What do you think "mono" means? And "di"?

Another way to tell monocots and dicots apart is to look at their later leaves. Look at the picture on page 55.

See how the tubes run into the leaves? In a monocot leaf, all the tubes run in the same direction. In a dicot leaf, the tubes run in many directions. Are the leaves monocot or dicot?

The stems of monocots and dicots are also different from each other. Monocots have soft, green stems which are sometimes hollow. Dicots have hard woody stems. Can you think of a soft-stemmed plant? What would a maple tree be?

A third way to tell the difference between monocots and dicots is to count the flower petals. Monocots have petals in groups of three (3, 6, 9, and so on). Dicots have petals in groups of four or five (4, 5, 8, 10, and so on). Look at the pictures below and decide which are monocots and which are dicots.

Study the chart below to compare monocots and dicots.

	Monocots	**Dicots**
Leaf Tubes	Go in the same direction	Go in all directions
No. of Flower Petals	Groups of 3	Groups of 4 or 5
No. of Seed Leaves	1	2
Stems	soft, hollow	woody

Look at the classification table to see how the plants have been classified.

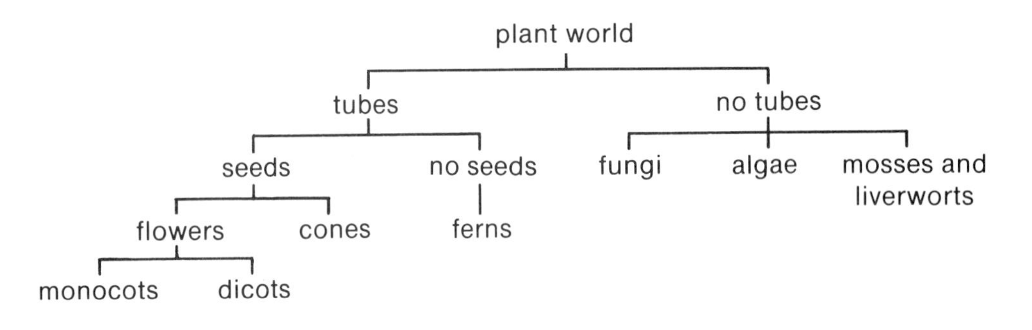

"As for man, his days are as grass: as a flower of the field, so he flourisheth." *Psalm 103:15*

Length, Area, and Volume

"And he that talked with me had a golden reed to measure the city, and the gates thereof, and the wall thereof.

And the city lieth foursquare, and the length is as large as the breadth: and he measured the city with the reed, twelve thousand furlongs. The length and the breadth and the height of it are equal." *Revelation 21:15 and 16*

Length

Suppose that you know that a hemlock tree is sixty feet tall. Without cutting it down, you could use that tree to measure distances along the ground. Can you think of a way to do that?

Try holding a pencil at arm's length. Line the pencil up with the edge of the chalkboard or the door frame, pencil point down. When the pencil just covers the edge of the chalkboard or the door frame, turn the pencil down parallel to the floor, keeping the point in the same place. How have you measured distance without moving any furniture? Could you use the sixty-foot tree in the same way?

How accurate do you think this kind of measuring is? If you used the tree as a tool for measuring, you might tell someone to bury a treasure three hemlock-tree lengths from a certain rock. That person would have to be sure to use the same tree you did. What else would he have to do just the way you did it? Would you be able to use the same method to find the treasure five years later? Why not?

What other ways are there of measuring length? How would you measure the length of your classroom? Would you measure the distance to your house in the same way? How would you report your findings?

Lord Kelvin, a British scientist who lived about 100 years ago, said that measurements must be expressed in numbers. Only then, he said, do you know something about what you are measuring.

Scientists make many kinds of measurements, and they try to make them as accurately as possible. All scientists use the same ways of measuring. Why do you think they do that? They can more easily share information and keep records.

The system you probably know best is the *English system.* It has units such as inches, feet, yards, miles, pints, quarts, gallons, and tons. These units are sometimes hard to multiply and divide and sometimes hard to remember. An easier system to use is the *metric system.* Scientists all over the world have agreed to use the metric system.

Measurements of length in this system begin with the *meter.* A meter is a little longer than a yard. 1,000 meters makes a *kilometer.* What do you think *kilo-* means?

Units smaller than a meter are the *centimeter* and the *millimeter.* Find out what *centi-* means. What part of a meter is a centimeter? Find out what *milli-* means. What part of a meter is a millimeter?

Which units would you use to measure your foot? Which would you use to measure a fly's wing? Which two would you probably use to measure your height?

If you have a string and a ruler you can find out how big around a soda can or a chair leg or even a cat is. Can you figure out how to measure around things that are not square?

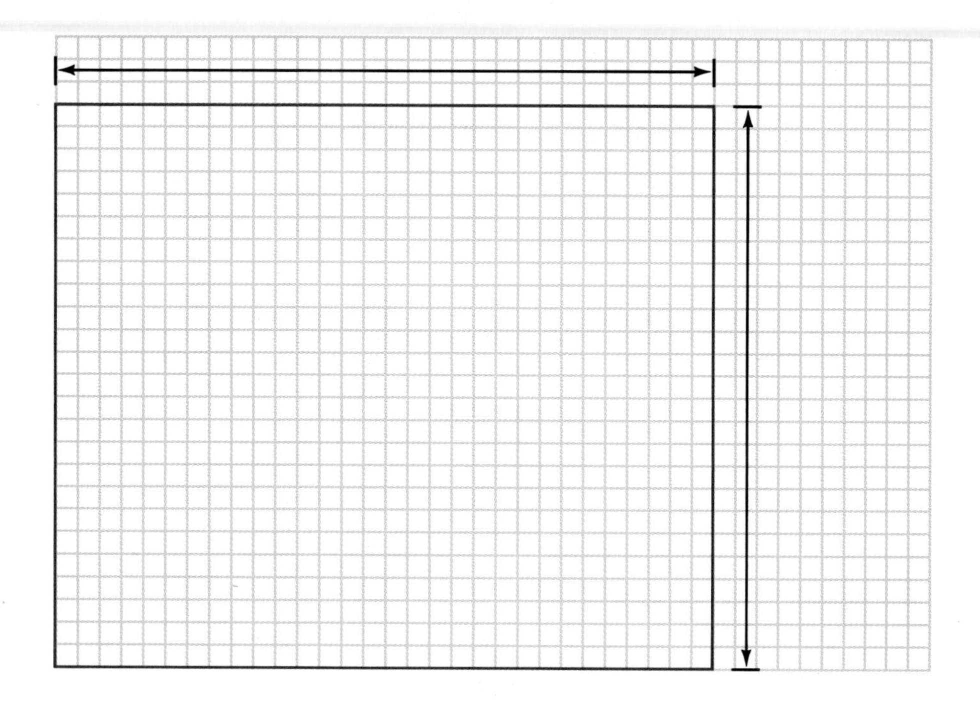

Area

How big is the front of your notebook? Do you know how to find out? The surface of the front of your notebook is the *area.* If you measure the width and the length and multiply those two measurements together, you will come up with the area of the notebook.

AREA= WIDTH × LENGTH

Suppose the notebook is twenty-five centimeters wide and thirty centimeters long. You need to multiply 25 by 30 to find the area. What is the answer? You should get the number 750. But 750 what? It cannot be centimeters because centimeters measure only along a line—not an area. We say a line is *one-dimensional;* it has only length. An area is *two-dimensional.* What does it have?

The area of the notebook is 750 *square centimeters.* Area is always expressed in square units.

If each block is one square centimeter, how many square centimeters are in these pictures?

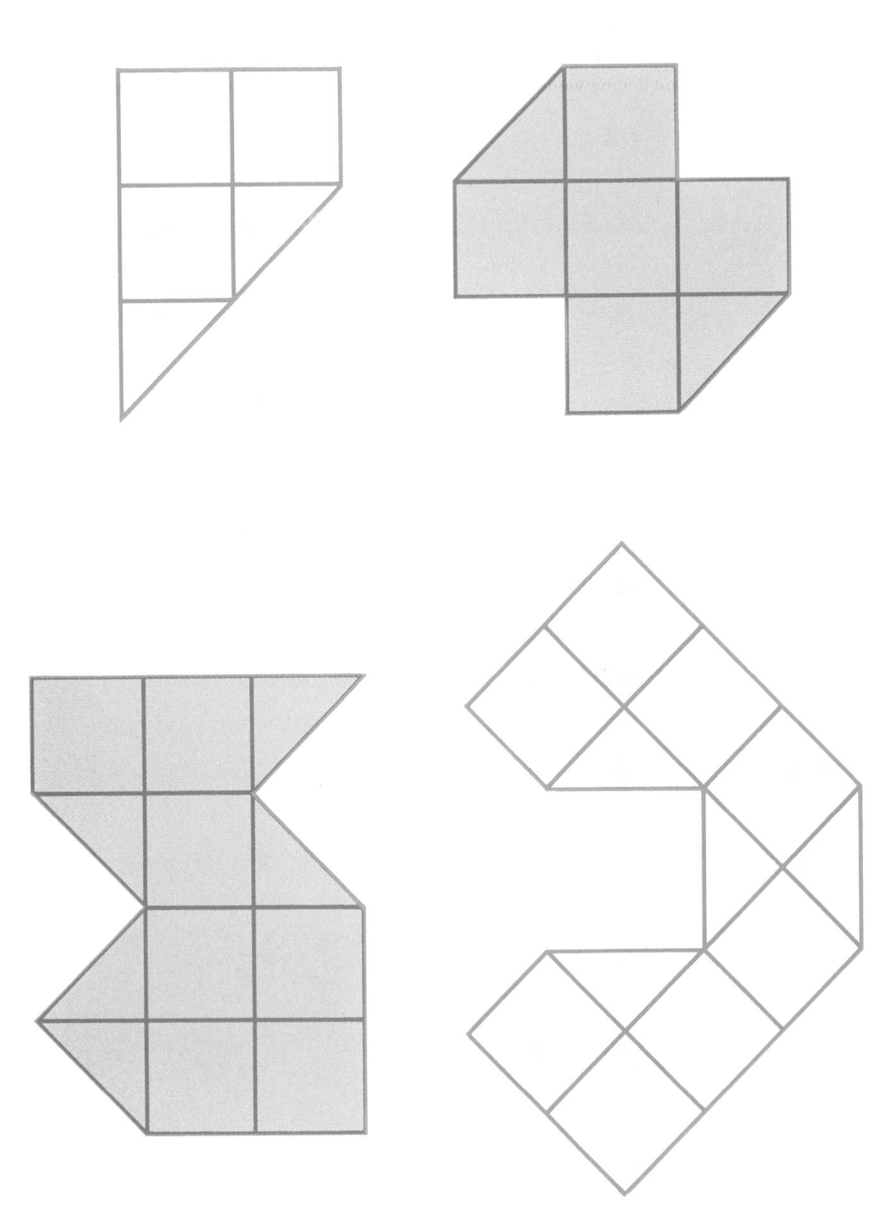

Finding Out . . .

About Length and Area

1. Get a ruler, a pencil, graph paper, and several flat objects to measure.
2. Measure the length and width of all the objects. Record your findings.
3. Draw around one of the flat objects on the graph paper. Determine the area represented on the graph paper. Now find the area by multiplying the length and width of the object. Record and compare your findings.

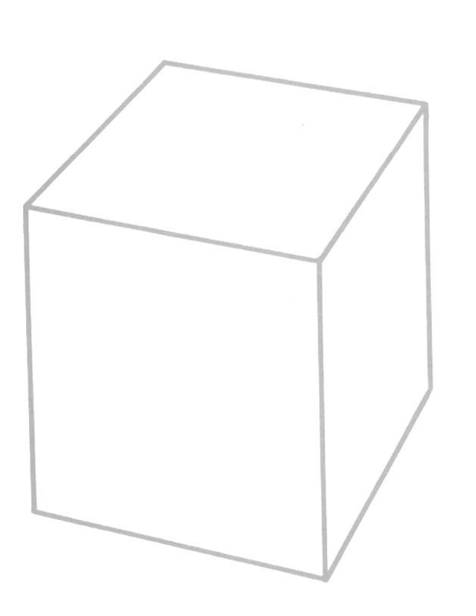

Volume

Which figure has three dimensions? Do you think you can find out how much space it takes up? The space it occupies is called its *volume*.

What does the three-dimensional figure have that the two-dimensional one does not? It has height or depth. What measurements do you think you multiply together to find the volume?

VOLUME = LENGTH × WIDTH × HEIGHT

If you have a box that is ten centimeters wide and ten centimeters high and twenty centimeters long, you have a box that has a volume of 2,000 *cubic centimeters.* Volume is always expressed in cubic units.

What would happen if you tried to multiply meters and centimeters? What would you get? To find volume or area, you have to use measurements expressed in the same units.

Not all objects have smooth, regular sides. How do you think you could find the volume of a stone? Or a gold crown? A mathematician in ancient Greece named Archimedes was given a similar problem.

King Hieron II had ordered an artist to make him a crown of pure gold. But when the crown arrived, the king suspected that the artist had cheated him. He asked Archimedes to find out whether the crown was pure gold without destroying the crown. Archimedes thought and thought about it. There seemed no way to test the gold without heating it or damaging the crown.

One day while sitting in a bath, Archimedes noticed that the water level went up when something was immersed in it. "Eureka!" he cried. He had found the answer. Do you know what it was?

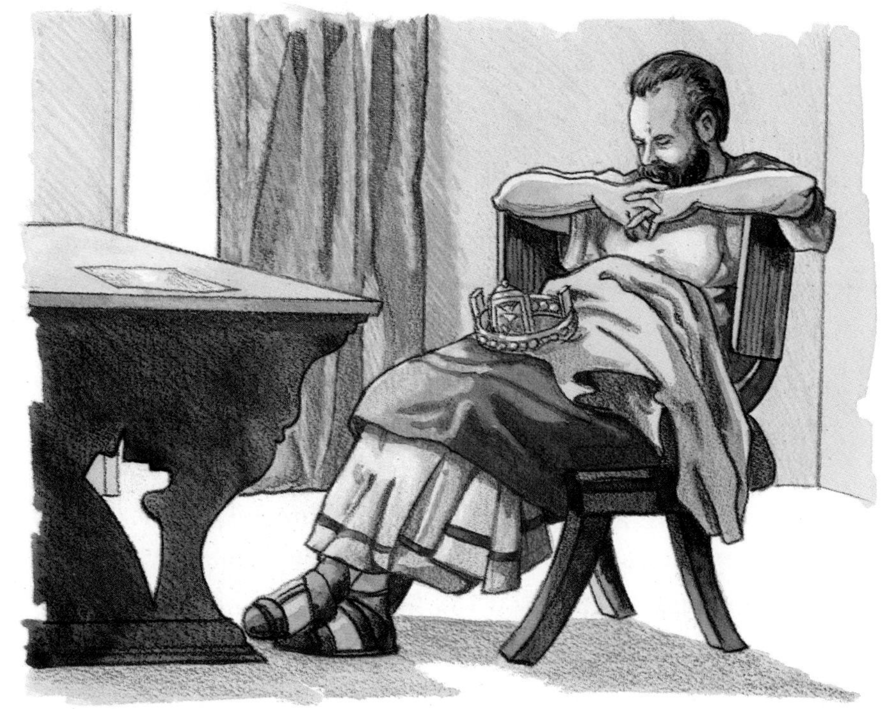

Archimedes took a piece of gold he knew was pure and immersed it in water. Then he measured how much water had been moved and weighed the water. By comparing the weight of the gold with the weight of the water that moved up when the gold was put in, he found out how much water real gold should move or *displace*.

The mathematician took the crown and tested it the same way. What do you think he found? He found that the artist had indeed cheated the king. He had kept some of the gold for himself and made part of the crown from silver.

Archimedes was looking for more than a simple volume with his test, but you can use the same idea to find the volume of objects that do not have smooth, easy-to-measure sides.

An object that is completely immersed in water will displace a volume of water that is the same as its own volume. Suppose you put water into a *graduated cylinder* until the lowest point is fifty cubic centimeters. Then you put in a small plastic toy. The lowest part of the water now is at fifty-seven cubic centimeters. What is the volume of the toy?

Finding Out . . .

About Volume

1. Get a graduated cylinder, water, and a small stone.
2. Pour some water into the cylinder. Take a reading at the lowest curved part of the surface of the water.
3. Place the stone into the water. Be sure the water completely covers the stone. Take another reading at the lowest curved part of the surface of the water.
4. Subtract the first reading from the second. Record the volume of the stone.

Digestion

Did you know your digestive system is rather like a factory? It takes in material, makes useful products, and distributes them. Some part of this factory is always operating, and rarely do the workers fail to do their work. The factory is one of the most efficient and inexpensive to operate. And what it produces for your body is extremely valuable.

What is your favorite food? Think of taking a bite of it right now. Just thinking about a food you like can set the first stage of digestion going. Looking at food or smelling it can also cause this process to begin. Can you guess what the first part of digestion is?

The Mouth

Glands in the cheeks near the ears and below the tongue pour *saliva* into the mouth. They produce about a quart of saliva a day. Without saliva, food would not get soft enough to swallow easily and you would not be able to taste anything. Even when you are not eating, saliva usually keeps your mouth moist inside.

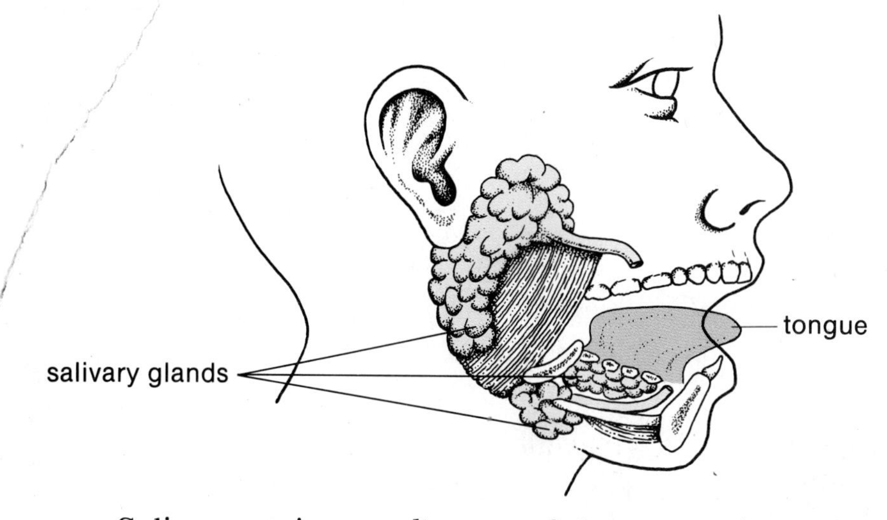

Saliva contains *ptyalin,* one of the many *enzymes* that glands in the body make to help digest food. Bread, potatoes, and corn are foods that ptyalin works on as you chew. It turns the starch in them into sugar. Meats and fats are not changed into sugar by saliva. But the more saliva any food has in it the better it forms a small ball, or *bolus,* for swallowing. Why do you think it is important to chew your food well before you swallow?

Your tongue and your teeth are also essential to good digestion. The tongue pushes food around inside the mouth; it moves the food so that the teeth can crush it into small pieces. The tongue also has another job, one you probably think is more important. It lets you taste your food.

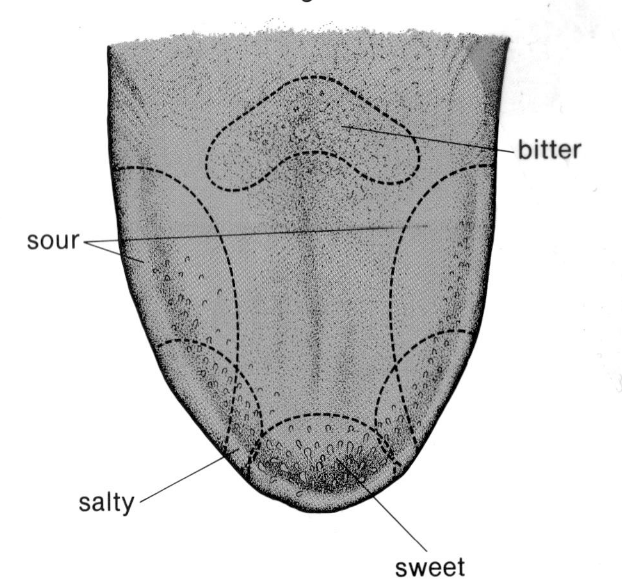

The tongue has about ten thousand *taste buds,* special organs that react to chemicals. The tongue can detect four kinds of taste: sweet, salty, sour, and bitter. Taste buds that pick up sweet flavors are on the tip of the tongue. Salty and sour detectors are usually along the sides; taste buds that react to bitter tastes are along the back. What else does your tongue help you do?

You need to take good care of your teeth because they bite and grind all the food you eat. The front teeth cut and tear; the side and back teeth grind and crush. If you do not care for your teeth, bits of food, saliva, dead cells, and bacteria will build up on them. As the bacteria grow in these conditions, they make an acid that eats holes, or *cavities,* into the enamel. Have you ever had a hole in your tooth filled? What did the dentist replace the enamel with?

When you decide you have chewed your food enough, the tongue forms it into a bolus and pushes it toward the back of your throat. Up until now, you could still spit the food out. But once you start to swallow, your body takes over and you must swallow.

The Throat

If you eat too fast or if you try to talk as you swallow, you may get something "down the wrong throat." What do you think that means? You really have only one throat, the *pharynx;* but it branches into a windpipe and a food pipe a little below the back of the mouth. The windpipe is called the *trachea,* and the food pipe is called the *esophagus.* Where the pharynx branches there is a valve that closes off the trachea when you swallow. If you swallow too fast, the valve sometimes does not get closed and some food goes down your trachea. Then what happens?

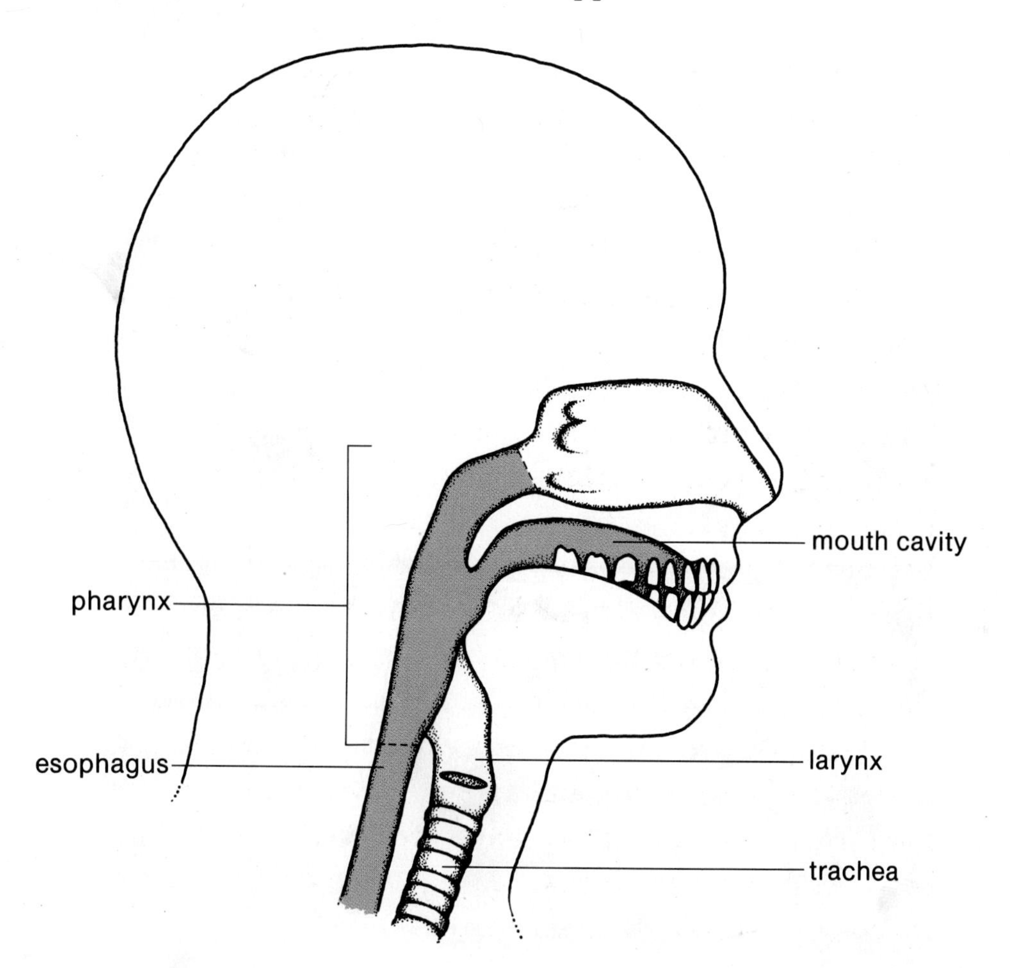

If food goes down your trachea, you cough. If the food completely blocks the trachea, you choke. Do you know what to do if someone cannot breathe because food has lodged in his windpipe? You should stand behind him and stretch your arms around him. Put your fist just below the middle of his ribs. Then, putting your other hand over your fist, press in quickly. The sudden rush of breath going out can move the food out of the trachea. You should never try this on your own. Let a trained adult help you.

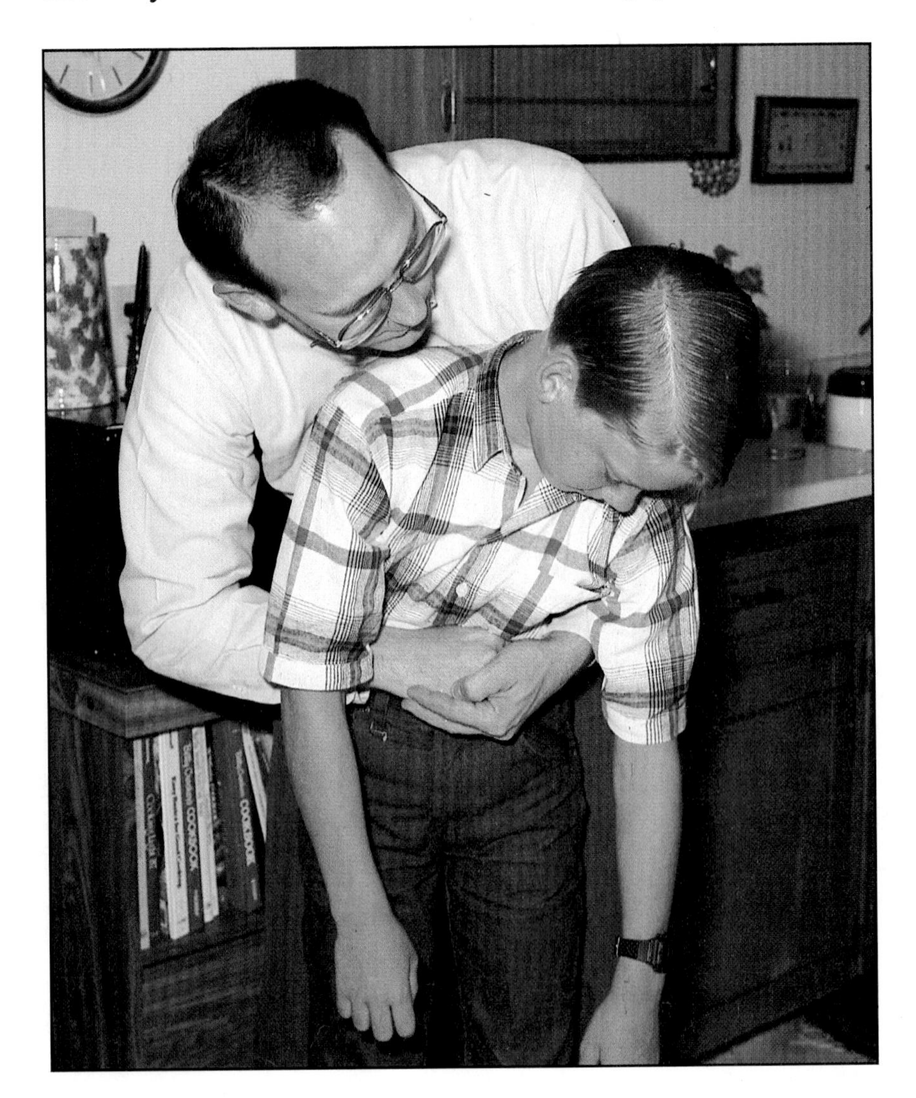

The esophagus is a short tube that carries food into your stomach. The esophagus has a tough lining that protects the muscles, and it can stretch wider than its normal size. Why are these two characteristics important for a food pipe?

The muscles of the esophagus contract in waves to move the food into the stomach. These muscles are so strong that you can swallow even while standing on your head. The movement of the muscles is called *peristalsis.* The name comes from two Latin word parts that mean "to wrap around." The muscles squeeze in above the bolus, pushing it along. The next group of muscles then squeeze in above the bolus and so on. The muscles continue to "wrap around" the food in this way until it passes into the stomach. The process is something like working a marble through a rubber hose by pinching the hose together above the marble.

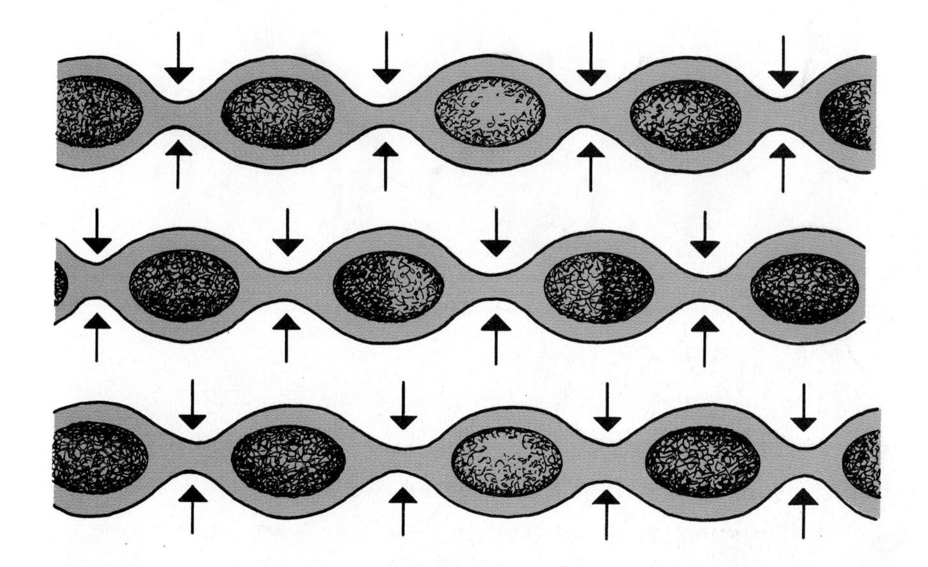

peristalsis

At the bottom of the esophagus are some strong muscles. They can pinch together. The opening these muscles control is called a *sphincter,* which comes from a word that means "to bind tightly." Is that a suitable name? Why does the food pipe need to be closed at the top of the stomach? Without such a valve, food might rise back up whenever you bend over, jump up, or eat too much.

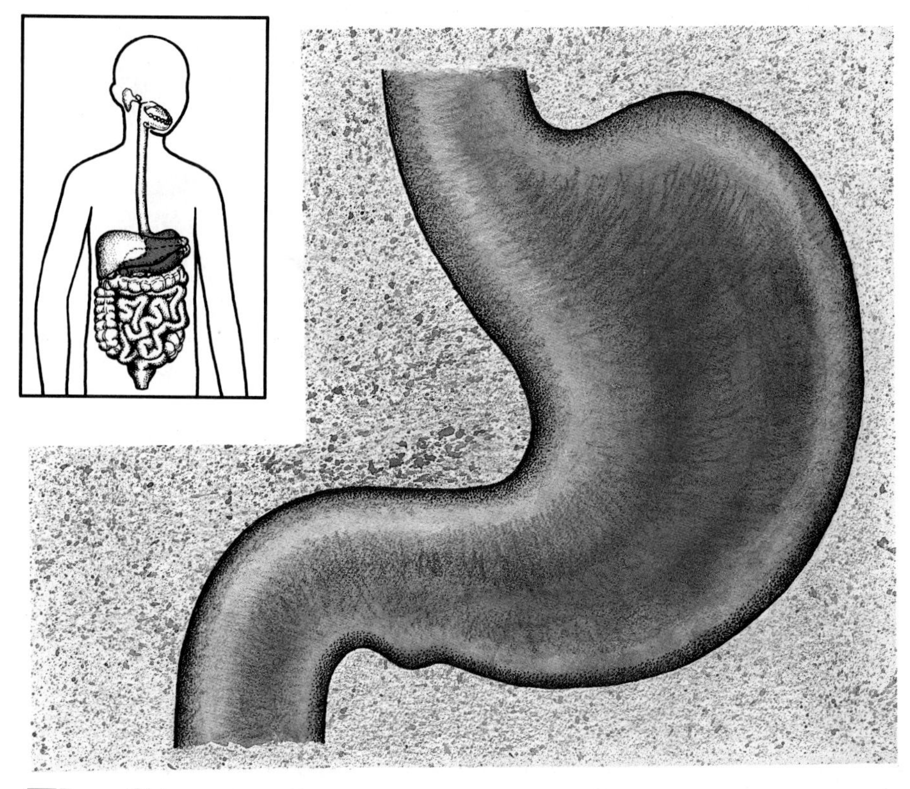

The Stomach

The stomach is probably the first thing you think of when you think of digestion. But as you can see, it does not function until digestion is well under way. Where do you think your stomach is?

Many people think that the stomach is right in the middle of the body. But it is higher, just below the ribs. It is about the size of your two fists. Did you think it was bigger than that?

The stomach is mostly a storage bag, a bulge in the food tube, that acts on food in the ways that the mouth does. What are the two ways that the mouth works on food? It works on it *mechanically* by moving it around, and it works on it *chemically,* changing and breaking food down into different parts.

Does your stomach growl sometimes? You probably say that you are hungry whenever that happens. But your stomach can rumble even when it has food in it. Your stomach churns food by peristalsis, the muscles around the middle and lower part squeezing much like the esophagus muscles. Because the stomach nearly always has some air, or gas, in it, the churning food sometimes sloshes about and creates a rumble.

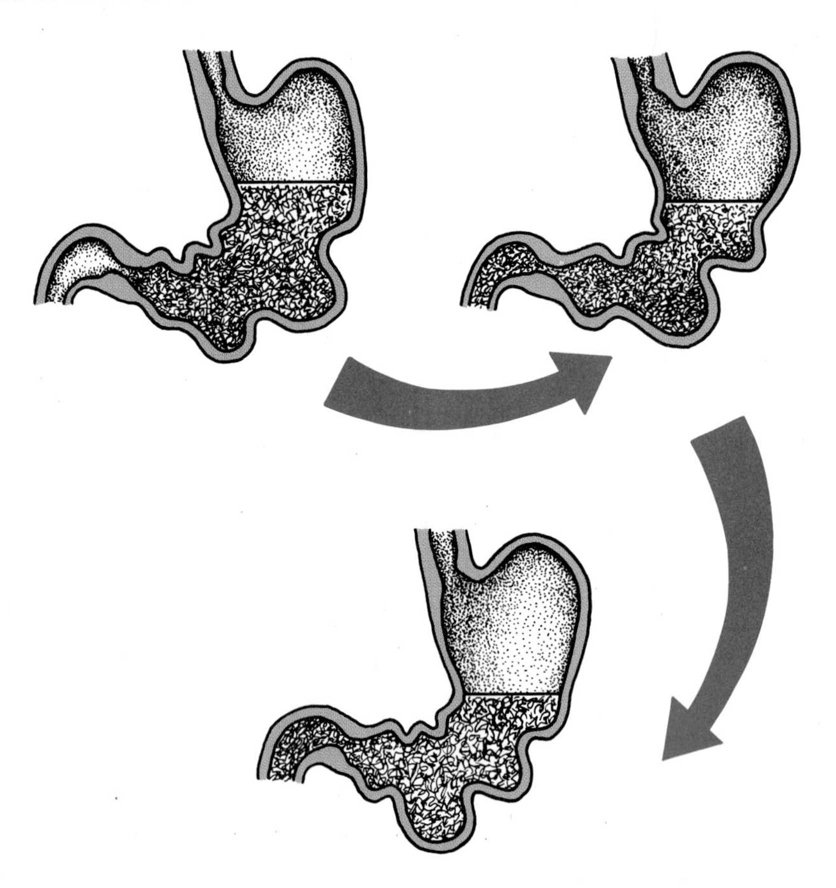

When you taste, smell, see, or even think about food, the glands that line your stomach start making *gastric juice,* a mixture of enzymes, water, and acid. The enzyme *pepsin* starts the digestion of proteins such as those in milk, meat, and fish. But pepsin cannot work unless it is in an acid.

The acid the stomach makes is *hydrochloric acid.* Besides making pepsin work, it kills some bacteria that you often swallow with food.

You may wonder what keeps the stomach acid from digesting the stomach itself. Many glands in the stomach produce a special coating that protects it. If too little coating is produced or if too much acid is produced, the acid can eat into the wall of the stomach. The pit or hole that is eaten out is called an *ulcer.* Worry and fear can cause the brain to tell the stomach to make more acid than is really needed. Why should you try to have a pleasant time at meals?

"Better is a dinner of herbs where love is, than a stalled ox and hatred therewith." *Proverbs 15:17*

The Intestines

Little by little the food that is now liquid leaves the bottom of the stomach through a valve called the *pyloric sphincter. Pyloric* comes from two Greek words that mean "gate watcher." What do you think the pyloric sphincter does? Regularly, the "gate watcher" opens and a spoonful of liquid food, or *chyme,* moves on to the next stage of digestion.

The *small intestine* is about twenty-three feet long, but it is narrow, only about an inch and a half across at the widest point. It has two layers of muscles that work together in peristalsis, keeping the chyme moving.

The intestine is lined on the inside with microscopic projections called *villi,* which look something like the strands on a shag rug. In fact, the inside of the intestine resembles deep-pile carpeting. How many villi do you think your small intestine has? It has about five million.

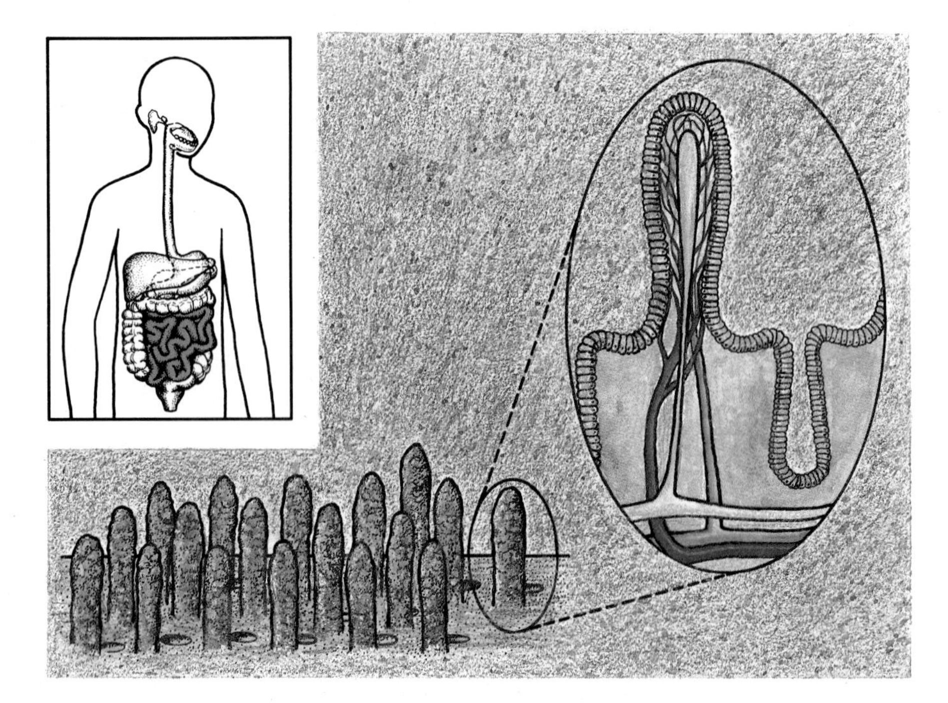

The villi have cells that absorb nutrients from the chyme as it passes through the intestine. Blood vessels in the villi pick up the nutrients. The food you ate earlier is now a part of the bloodstream.

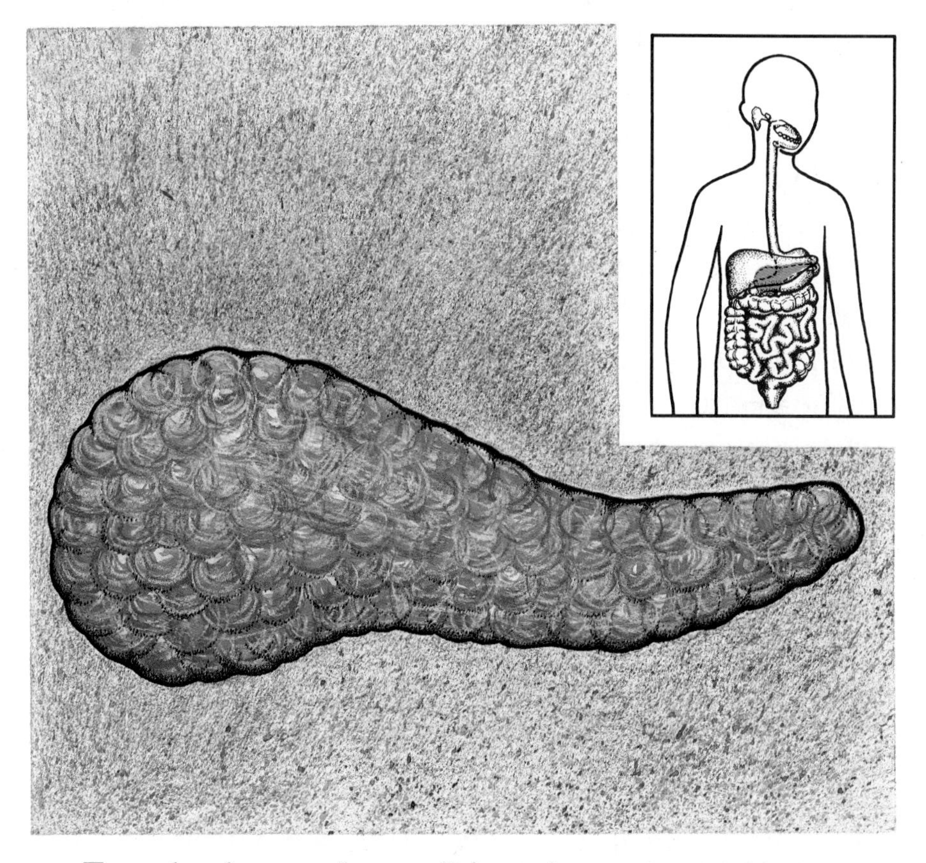

Two glands near the small intestine put out substances that cause food to continue breaking down. The *pancreas* makes three enzymes that act on starches, proteins, and fats. It also produces *insulin.* Insulin makes the body's cells able to use the sugar that is absorbed into the bloodstream.

If there is not enough insulin in the bloodstream, a disease called *diabetes mellitus* results. How does diabetes mellitus interfere with digestion? People with diabetes can eat special foods and take insulin so that they can keep the right amount of sugar in their blood.

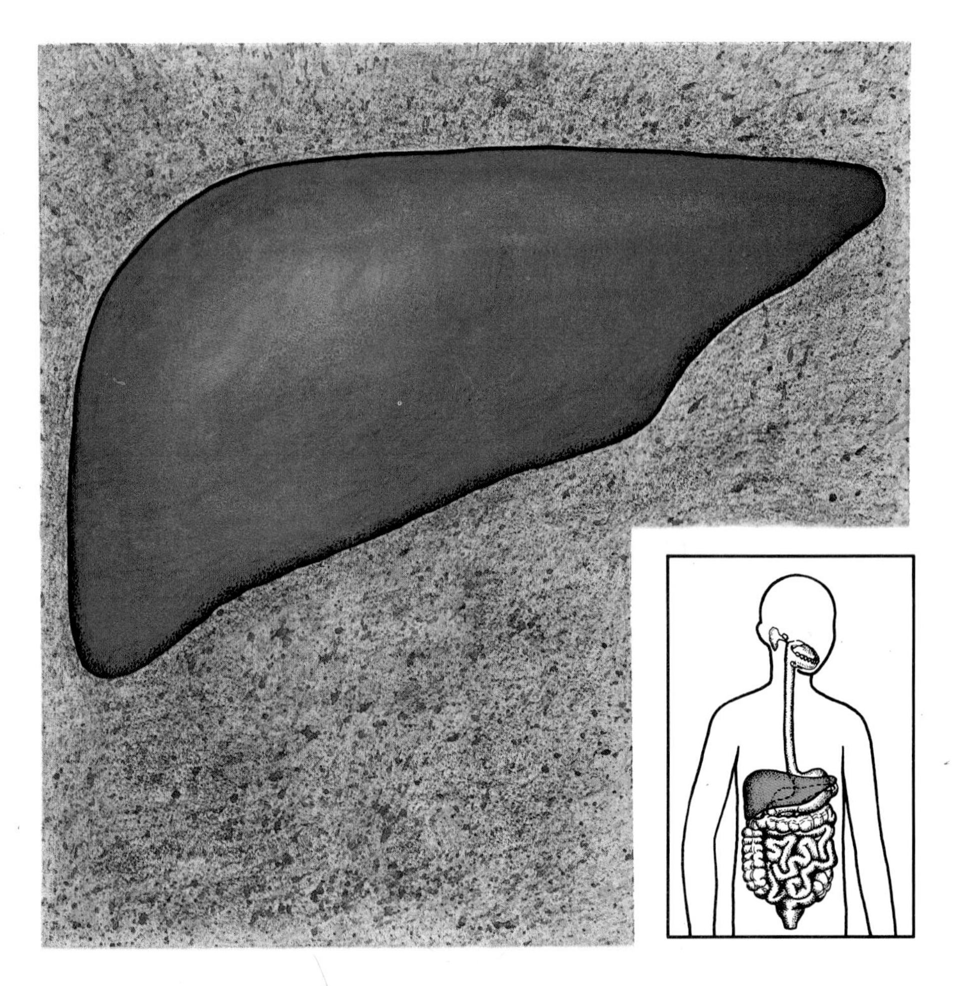

The liver also works on poisons that get into the bloodstream. It *neutralizes* poisons or makes them harmless. Drugs and alcohol are poisons. If the liver has to deal with too much poison, it becomes diseased. Then it is unable to perform many of its important jobs.

The liver is a big gland that has 500 different functions that we know of. One thing it does is produce *bile,* a green liquid that helps break down fats. Bile works on fats much like dish-washing detergent works on grease. Do oil and water mix very well? How does detergent change the oil? What do you think bile does to fats? Bile also helps the body absorb vitamins.

After the chyme passes through the small intestine, it goes into the *large intestine.* The large intestine absorbs water and salts. Digestion is now complete. Any fiber or material that the body did not digest travels through the rest of the large intestine and is eliminated as waste.

Our bodies need vitamins, minerals, proteins, and sugars to operate well and to stay healthy. What you eat is extremely important. All that your body has to work with comes from the food you choose. Proteins build muscle cells; fats provide energy; minerals build bones, teeth, and blood. Sugars provide energy, but they are quickly used up. If you eat a variety of good foods, you will probably be giving your body what it needs.

Staying healthy is not the only reason people eat. Eating is also enjoyable. The four main tastes combine into thousands of delightful sensations for your mouth. And people enjoy being together when they eat, enjoying one another's company. In fact, the word *companion,* meaning "friend," comes from Latin words that mean "to take bread together."

"Neither have I gone back from the commandment of his lips; I have esteemed the words of his mouth more than my necessary food." *Job 23:12*

Finding Out . . .

About Taste

1. Get a clean, dry towel, some salt, some lemon juice, some sugar, and a package of unsweetened Kool-Aid.
2. Dry off your tongue with the towel.
3. Let your teacher put some sugar on your tongue. Can you taste it?
4. Now let saliva cover your tongue. Do you taste the sugar now?
5. Let your teacher put some lemon juice on the tip of your tongue. Can you taste it? Try the other foods on different places on your tongue. Can you find the taste areas on your tongue?
6. Record your observations.

The Moon's Structure and Motions

The Structure of the Moon

Have you ever looked for "the man in the moon"? Some people think the dark places on a full moon look like a face. What do you think those eyes and nose and mouth really are?

The Surface of the Moon

A long time ago, people thought that the moon had continents and oceans much like the earth has. They assumed that the dark places on the surface were water. They named the dark spots *maria,* meaning lunar "seas." We know now that these are not seas at all, but large plains shaped much like circles. There are about thirty maria on the side of the moon facing us. The one in the middle is called Mare Imbrium. It is about 1,100 km (700 mi) across.

Besides the flat regions, the moon also has mountains and mountain ranges, named like mountains on earth. There are more mountains in the southern hemisphere of the moon than in the northern hemisphere. Some of the mountains are more than 7,500 meters (25,000 ft) high—almost five miles high! How do you think the mountains on the moon differ from the mountains on earth? How do wind and water change the earth's mountains? How do the mountains on the moon look? Why?

Probably the most famous features of the moon are its many craters. The word *crater* comes from the Greek word for "cup" or "bowl-shaped." How is a crater like a cup or a bowl? Some craters have light streaks called *rays* that spread out in all directions. One crater with such rays is called Tycho. During a full moon these rays look like the top of a peeled orange.

Many other craters are surrounded by steep walls that rise high above the moon's surface, some as much as 6,000 meters (20,000 ft.) above the bottom of the crater. The moon's craters look somewhat like the craters on earth that were formed by volcanoes.

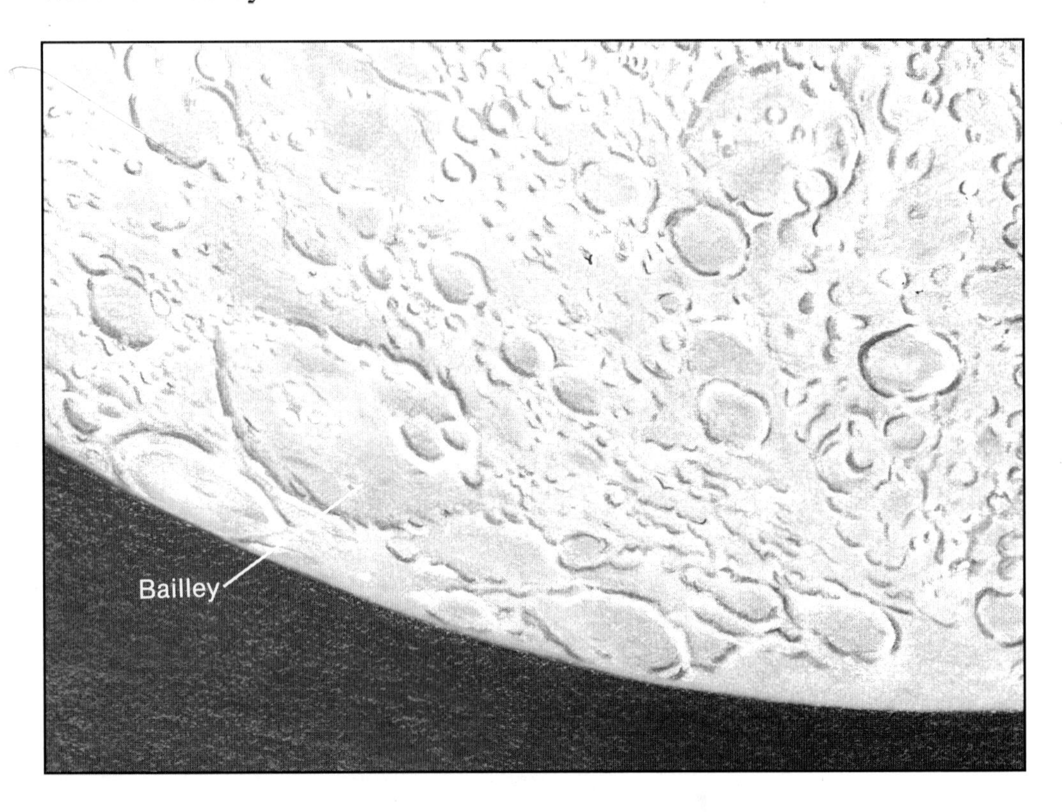

Observers have counted at least 30,000 craters on the moon. Some areas have so many craters that they overlap. Craters range in size from as small as a soup bowl to so large that it would take ten hours at sixty miles an hour to drive around the rim. Bailley is the moon's largest crater, being 295 km (183 mi) across.

Scientists think that most of the moon's craters were formed when meteors hit its surface. They collided with the moon at great speeds and exploded. The great explosions caused craters much bigger than the meteors themselves.

Some craters may have formed like volcanic craters form on the earth. Gases from the interior of the moon escape through cracks in the moon's surface. The gases then expand because there is no atmosphere to keep them contained. The expanding gases tear away the moon's surface material, causing craters.

A fourth feature of the moon is the cracks, called *rills.* These canyonlike valleys that run along the lunar surface may be straight or curved. They are from a few feet to three miles wide, and some are hundreds of miles long. Most scientists believe moonquakes caused the rills. What do you suppose a moonquake is like?

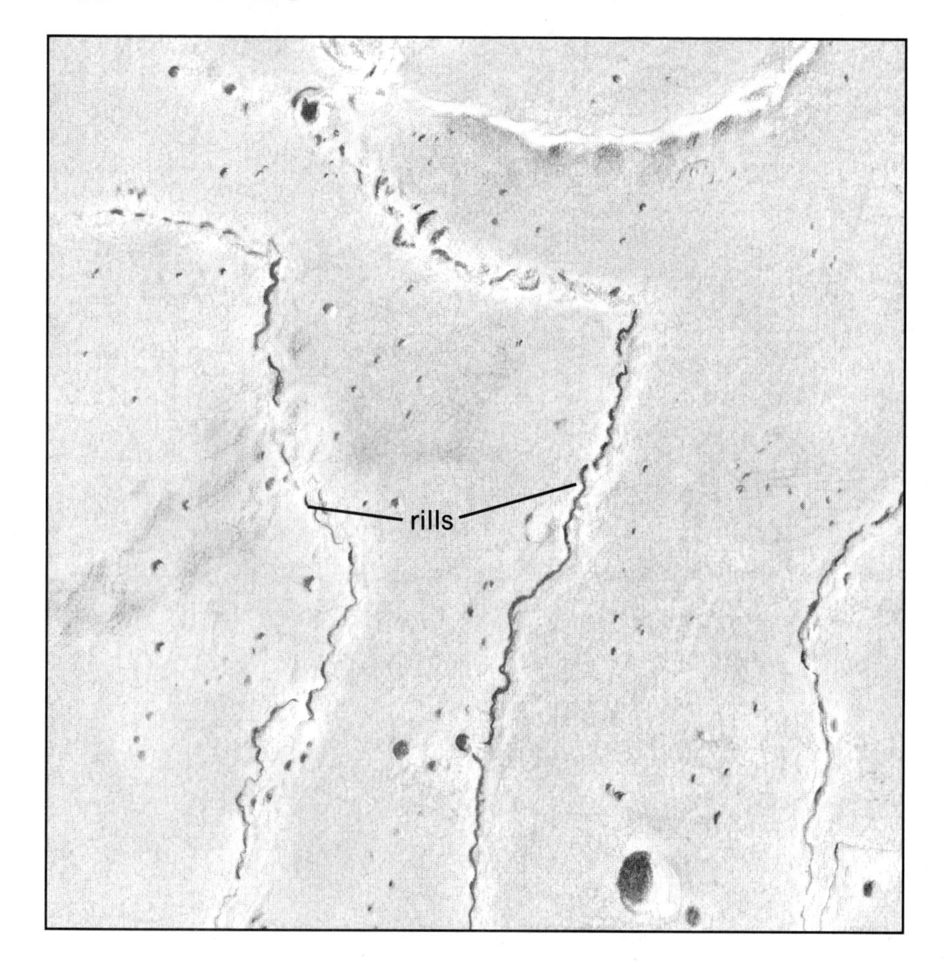

The Size of the Moon

You already know that the moon is smaller than the earth. But do you know how much smaller? The moon is about 3,500 km (2,160 mi) across, about one-fourth the earth's diameter. If the moon were dropped into the Atlantic Ocean, one side of it would touch eastern Canada and the other side would touch Europe. Imagine the splash that would make!

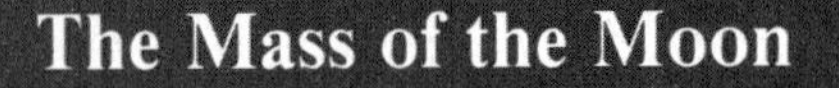

The Mass of the Moon

Mass, you probably remember, is how much matter something has. Two things may be the same size but have different masses. A styrofoam ball may be the same size as a softball, but it has less matter. The mass of an object does not change, even in space.

How does the moon's mass compare to earth's? Its mass is about one-eightieth the mass of the earth's. That means that the earth has eighty times more matter than the moon does.

The Gravity of the Moon

Although the mass of an object does not change in different places, its weight can. How can this be? Weight depends on gravity, but mass does not. The more pull of gravity there is on an object the more the object will weigh. Do you think you would weigh the same on the moon as on the earth?

Your mass is the same on the moon and the earth, but your weight is different. The gravity on the moon is about one-sixth of that on earth. This means that if you weigh sixty-six pounds on earth, you would weigh eleven pounds on the moon.

How would the gravity on the moon change your ability to play sports? A high jumper who can jump six-and-a-half feet on earth could jump thirty-nine feet high on the moon. Imagine being able to jump up to look into a third-story window! If you can hit a baseball 400 feet on earth, you could hit the same ball almost a half mile on the moon.

The Shape of the Moon

Although the earth and the moon are both ball-shaped, neither is *perfectly* round. The slower an object spins the more nearly round it is. A planet that spins fast will be slightly wider around the equator. The earth spins around once in twenty-four hours. The moon spins around once in about twenty-eight days. Which body spins faster? Which is more nearly round—the earth or the moon?

The Distance of the Moon from the Earth

The path the moon takes around the earth is not perfectly round. What is the path called? It is an *ellipse.*

Look at the diagram of the positions of the moon. Is the moon the same distance from the earth in A as it is in B? Because this distance changes as the moon goes around the earth, we talk about the moon's average distance from the earth. This distance is halfway between its closest and farthest points from the earth.

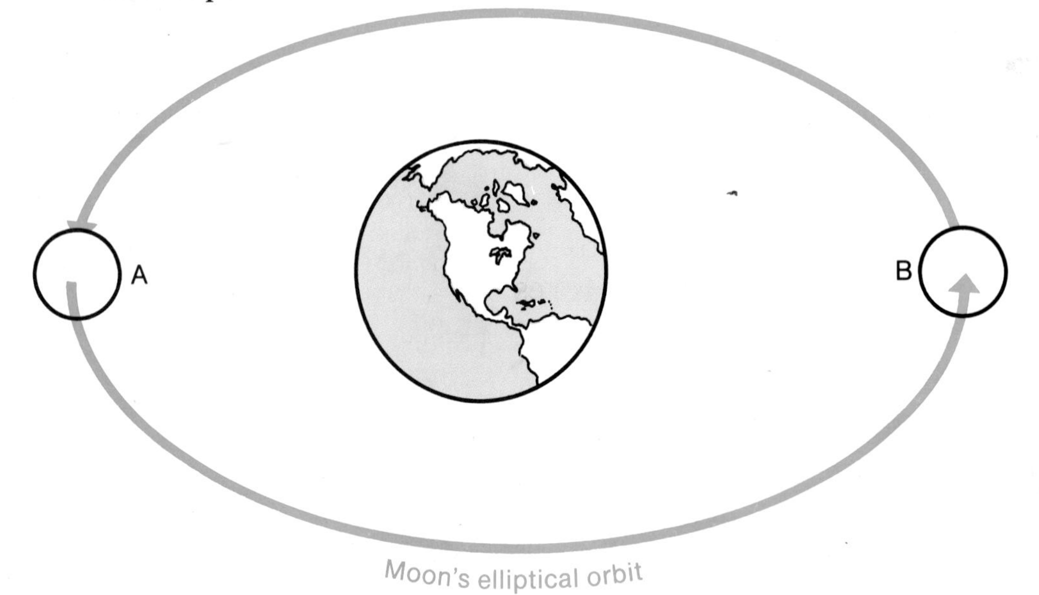

Moon's elliptical orbit

The average distance between the moon and the earth is 385,000 km (239,000 mi). To travel this distance on earth you would have to go around the earth more than nine-and-a-half times. If you would show every mile from here to the moon as one inch, how many inches away would you place the moon on this scale?

You would need enough inches to equal almost four miles!

The Moon's Temperatures

Do you think the moon is colder or warmer than the earth? If you guessed colder, you are right. But if you guessed warmer you are also right. There are greater variations in surface temperatures on the moon than there are on earth. Why is this so? What causes temperatures on earth to vary less than the temperatures on the moon? Our atmosphere acts as an insulator to keep temperatures about the same.

The moon orbits the earth completely about once every 29 $\frac{1}{2}$ days. If you could stay in the same place on the moon for a month, you would be in light for half of that time (14 $\frac{3}{4}$ days).

During a moon day the temperature may reach 260° F. The night, though, may bring temperatures as low as -280° F. Without an atmosphere like the earth's, the moon is unable to trap heat. As soon as one side turns away from the sun, it immediately cools off. This changing temperature is called *surface temperature.* The moon also has a *stable temperature,* the temperature of its core.

The Moon's Motions

Revolution

What causes the moon to travel in an ellipse? Why doesn't the moon shoot off by itself into space? You already know that the force of gravity helps to keep the moon in its proper path. The force of gravity pulls you toward the earth. It also causes objects thrown into the air to fall back to the ground. This same force is pulling the moon toward earth. But why doesn't the moon crash into the earth?

There is another force that is acting on the moon, keeping it in orbit. This other force, called *inertia,* is the tendency of an object to stay in one place or to keep moving in a straight line. Suppose you rolled a bowling ball down a lane. What happens to the ball when you roll it perfectly straight? Inertia is the force that keeps the ball going toward the pins once you let the ball go.

Finding Out . . .

About Inertia

1. You will need a heavy but soft object (like a large stuffed animal) and a rope.
2. Go outside. Tie the object to a rope about four feet long. Swing the rope around your head so that the object goes in a circular path. What would happen to the object if the rope were cut? In which direction would the object travel? Let go of the rope. Watch to see the direction that the object travels.
3. The object flying off represents the force of inertia. What represents the force of gravity?
4. In your notebook, draw diagrams of how the moon might travel without the forces of gravity and inertia.

Pretend you are looking down onto the earth and the moon from space. In which direction do you think the moon revolves around the earth, clockwise or counterclockwise? How does this direction compare with the earth's revolution around the sun? Do you think it is the same? The moon orbits the earth counterclockwise; the earth orbits the sun in the same direction. The other planets revolve around the sun in the same counterclockwise direction. What can you say about the design of God's universe?

The moon revolves around the earth at the speed of about 3,500 km (2,200 mi) per hour. At this speed the moon travels over one-half mile in one second.

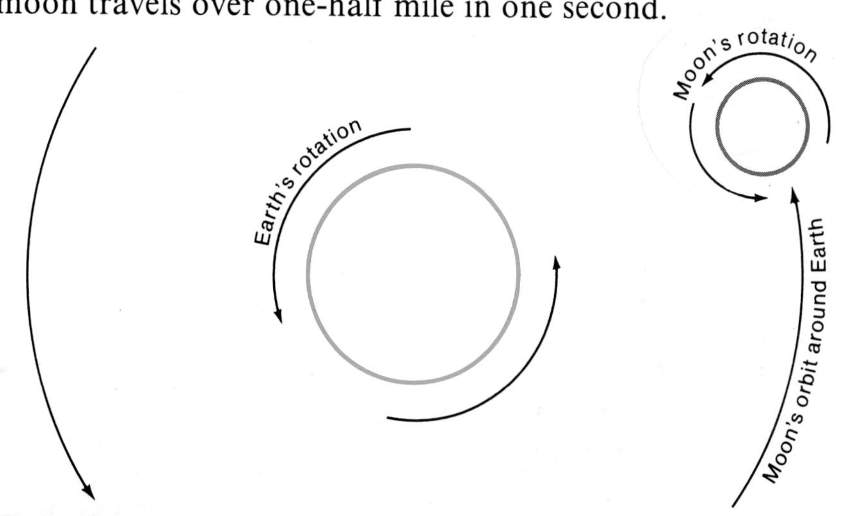

Rotation

The moon also spins or turns as it revolves around the sun. We call this spinning motion its *rotation.*

The moon takes as long to turn around once as it does to travel around the earth. How long does the moon take to go completely around the earth once? Then how long does it take to rotate once?

Do you think men can ever see the back of the moon from earth? Why not?

The Moon's Phases

If you look into the sky at different times during the month, you will notice that the moon can look like a ball, a banana, or a half circle. These shapes that the moon takes are called *phases.* What causes the moon to take these different shapes? As the moon travels in its orbit we see different portions of its lighted surface. The positions of the moon and earth to the sun determine what shape the moon seems to take.

This is how the moon, earth, and sun look from space. Notice that the sun always lights half the moon. Can you always see the lighted side of the moon? Why not? During the day it is hard to see the moon because the sun is so bright that it outshines the moon. The moon can best be seen at night or early in the morning or evening.

Have you ever heard someone speak of the "new moon"? If there is such a thing, what happens to the old moon? There is really only one moon. Every time it completes one revolution we call it a new moon. You cannot see the new moon because the moon is directly between the earth and the sun, and its dark side is facing the earth.

As the moon continues in its orbit a few days, you can begin to see a little of the moon's lighted side. It is called a *crescent* and is shaped something like a banana. About one week after the new moon, you can see half of the lighted side. This phase is called the first quarter. In a few more days you can see almost all of the moon's lighted surface seen from earth. At this phase the moon is called *gibbous,* meaning "humpbacked." Does it look like it has a curved or humped back to you?

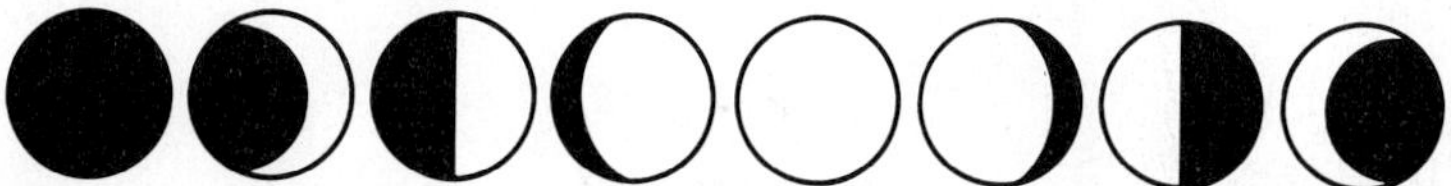

When the earth is between the sun and the moon, the sun shines on the moon's surface so that we can see all of its lighted surface. The full moon appears about two weeks after the new moon. When the moon goes from new moon to full moon the amount of lighted surface we see becomes larger. We say that the moon is *waxing,* or showing more of its lighted surface.

What happens to the moon after it passes through the phase of full moon? A few days after the last quarter, the moon becomes a crescent again. Finally, the moon completes its journey around earth, and there is a new moon once again. What happens to the lighted surface of the moon from full moon to new moon? The moon is *waning,* meaning that the lighted surface we see is getting smaller.

"Then spake Joshua to the Lord in the day when the Lord delivered up the Amorites before the children of Israel, and he said in the sight of Israel, Sun, stand thou still upon Gibeon; and thou, Moon, in the valley of Ajalon. And the sun stood still, and the moon stayed, until the people had avenged themselves upon their enemies." Joshua 10:12-13

Animal Defenses

"But I will sing of thy power; yea, I will sing aloud of thy mercy in the morning: for thou hast been my defence and refuge in the day of my trouble." *Psalm 59:16*

In the days of jousts and crusades, knights buckled on their armor and, astride great war horses, rode into battle to defend their land, their honor, and their king.

Every day, on a smaller scale, jousts and battles of a sort go on in the animal kingdom. Rhinos in their armor, porcupines with their spear-sharp spines, and caribou with their antlers hard as lances ward off enemies, defend their young, and protect their territories. The clank and crash of combat may resound through the wilderness when two bighorn sheep slam together head-on, or it can be as subtle and quiet as a snail pulling into its shell. But every confrontation is serious business, often a matter of life and death.

Built-in Defenses

God designed each animal with the equipment and behavior it needs for survival. The equipment for protecting, or built-in defenses, includes special colors or shapes, weapons, and protective coverings. Animals do different things to defend themselves. These actions of defense are known as *tactics.*

Special Colors or Shapes

These butterflies are hard to tell apart at first—or even second—glance. The appearance of the viceroy mimics, or looks like, the appearance of the monarch. Since monarchs are poisonous—and any bird that has tasted one knows it—the viceroy, because it looks like the distasteful monarch, is often left alone by experienced birds. We call this "looking alike" *mimicry.*

Sometimes instead of looking like other animals, animals are colored or shaped to look like their environment. This is a technique that soldiers sometimes use when they dress in mottled green clothes: *camouflage*. Camouflage helps conceal an animal.

One of these insects is a walking stick. Which one is it? Where do you think it spends most of its life? Can you see the one called a dead-leaf grasshopper? With its oddly shaped legs, it looks like brown leaves. In what ways does this camouflage protect the grasshopper?

Fawns of white-tailed deer have white spots on their coats. Since they cannot run well when they are very young, their mothers put them in a safe place and make them lie down. In tall grass or in the dappled light of the woods, fawns are hard to see.

One kind of lizard, called a chameleon, changes color from green to brown, depending on the surroundings. Found only in Africa and Asia, true chameleons can blend in with bark or leaves, sand, or grass. In what ways does this ability help the chameleon?

Finding Out . . .

About Camouflage

1. Get one sheet of red construction paper, one blue sheet, one green sheet, a hole puncher, a stop watch, a pair of scissors, and a plastic margarine container.

2. Cut the pieces of construction paper in half horizontally. Lay one half of each color on a table or on the floor. Punch holes from the other half sheets and collect them in the container.

3. Stir the confetti so that all the colors are mixed well. Then sprinkle a handful over the red sheet.

4. Giving yourself five seconds, count as many red dots as you can. Gather the confetti, sprinkle out another handful, and count as many blue dots as you can in five seconds. Repeat with the other colors. Record your findings.

Other animals' colors and shapes do not conceal them, but reveal them. Their appearance can frighten or warn other animals that to eat them may be painful or even deadly.

What might keep a bird from eating this moth? What might make a bird find this beetle unappetizing? Do these caterpillars look edible?

Weapons

Animals also have body parts, or *appendages* that help them defend themselves. What weapons do you see here?

Teeth, beaks, claws, hooves, tails, horns, antlers, and pincers are some of the weapons. Do animals have one weapon each, or do some animals have many? Can you think of an animal that has three of these kinds of weapons?

Antlers are bony growths that are shed every year. Horns are not shed; they are a bony structure with a layer of *keratin,* something like fingernails, that continues to grow and get bigger. Moose and elk, for example, have antlers; cows and bighorn sheep have horns.

Protective Coverings

Some animals wear armor. A snail, for example, has a hard shell to pull into. Others, like the rhinoceros and the armadillo, have tough hides. The rhinoceros also has another method of defense. What is it?

The name *armadillo* comes from a Spanish word for "armored." Armadillos are covered all over—except for the ears and feet—by tough plates. Young armadillos have leathery skin which hardens into a kind of armor by the time they are adults. Some kinds in South America can curl up, making one round ball of protection. North American armadillos dig holes or run into thorny bushes to escape predators. Why are these good defenses for the armadillo?

Other animals have stiff spines all over, like the porcupine. Porcupines do not "throw" their spines, as some people think. They raise the spines up and out, sticking any enemy that comes too close.

The sea urchin has spines all around its body. Some kinds of urchins have poison in the tips of the spines. One variety has small, tough plates around the spines where they join the body, allowing movement in any direction while protecting the muscle.

Special Defenses

There are some animals that release chemicals and use electricity to defend themselves. This beetle sprays a toxic liquid that provides a smokescreen and can stain human skin. It is the Bombardier beetle. Poisonous tree frogs in the tropics are brightly colored and boldly marked. What defense are their showy skins warning of?

One kind of eel, the electric eel, can deliver a 500-volt surprise to an attacker. There are nearly 500 kinds of fish and eels that generate varying amounts of electricity.

Tactics

Animals have many built-in defenses. But they also have many tactics that help them survive.

Sometimes the simplest thing to do is *hide.* Many animals use this tactic, and some use it almost exclusively. Have you ever seen a mouse in your house? If it saw *you,* it undoubtedly slipped under the nearest piece of furniture. Its response to danger was to hide.

Other animals *run* or *jump* to safety. Antelopes, kangaroos, jackrabbits, white-tailed deer, and springboks are fleet of foot and hoof and can often outrun their pursuers. Birds and bats can *fly* away (and a few squirrels and fishes can glide or sail briefly through the air). Most lizards can zip away from enemies; some also have tails that come off and keep wiggling in the predator's mouth while the lizard gets away. What kind of defense would you call that?

Another tactic of animals is to *group together.* Many kinds of fish travel in groups called *schools.* Any one of the fish in a school can change the direction of all by a sudden movement. The school has as many sensors for danger as it has members. Does this help you understand the old saying, "There is safety in numbers"?

You may think an elephant is so big that it has no enemies. But large cats like lions will attack a lone elephant. A herd of elephants, however, is safe. The herd can protect even the young and the sick from predators. What other defenses do elephants have?

Some animals are good at *bluffing.* Perhaps you have seen a house cat hissing at a dog. The cat's fur is bushed, even on its tail. The cat looks bigger, more threatening than usual—it's bluffing. An opossum has a different bluff. Instead of trying to scare its attacker, the opossum drops down as if dead. This defense often works because many predators will not eat what they have not killed.

Finding Out . . .

About Defenses

1. Study the following scenes or examples.
2. Tell what built-in defense or tactic the animal is using in each case.
3. Record your answers.

This bird lives in a snowy region. It has brown feathers in the summer and white ones in the winter. What is the ptarmigan's defense?

What does a turtle do when something taps its shell? What is the turtle's defense?

The coral snake is deadly. How does that fact help the king snake?

This fish is a puffer; it puffs up and looks bigger. What defense is this?

A skunk has stripes to warn off predators. But it is more famous for another kind of defense. What kind of defense is that?

Still other animals *put on disguises.* The decorator spider, for example, gathers up bits of leaves, sticking them to itself. This behavior makes it look like a flower on a plant.

The decorator crab does much the same thing, except it does it underwater. The salivary glands of this crab produce a sticky substance that holds even in salt water. The crab finds bits of coral, seaweed, and even rocks and attaches them all over its back and legs. Sometimes the crab uses living coral which continues to grow. Soon the crab looks like a moving forest of coral.

Since crabs *molt,* or lose their shells, the decorator crab has to replace its disguise several times in its life. Also, when the crab moves to a different place, it changes its covering, using items from the new environment. Why is that important?

Light

Imagine you are in a spaceship far from earth. The light of our sun now reaches you as a mere pinprick. The nearer stars dazzle you with their rich red and orange and white lights. The space between the stars is a velvet black; the planets you pass are purple, pink, and green. The lights and colors of outer space at first surprised you. But now the sights are familiar, like the skies of earth used to be. What makes all this light and dark, all this color, all this beauty?

What is Light?

Light is energy, waves of *radiant energy* from the sun and other sources. There are many kinds of radiant energy: radio waves, X-rays, ultraviolet rays, gamma rays, and more. Light rays, however, are the only ones that humans can see.

All the waves travel forward at the same speed—300,000 kilometers (186,000 mi) a second. They also move up and down as they travel forward, making waves. These waves are different lengths (*wavelengths*). The number of waves that pass by a point in a second is called the *frequency.* X-rays have a high frequency. What does that mean?

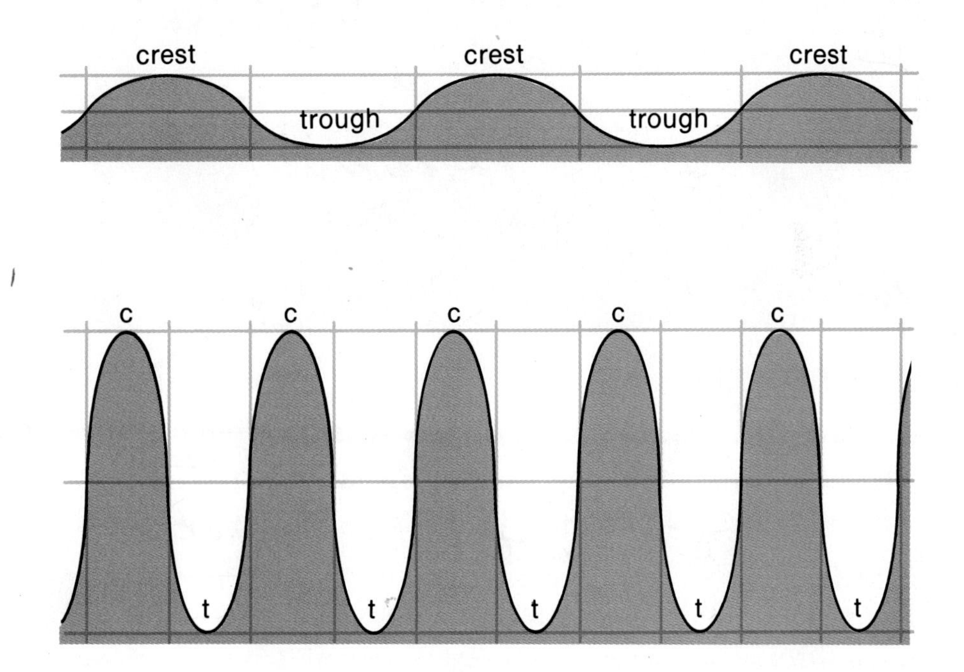

Where Light Comes From

Some materials produce energy that we see as light. The sun and the stars make such energy. They are natural sources of light. Some light sources are manmade, like electric bulbs, candles, and kerosene lamps. Anything—natural or manmade—that gives off its own light is *luminous*. Is fire a natural source of light? How about a lightning bug?

How Light Acts

Have you ever seen light bend itself to go around a corner? Light cannot bend itself; it travels in a straight line from its source. Would there be any shadows if light could bend?

Perhaps you have seen straight lines of light coming down through the trees in a forest, streaming in through church windows, or slicing through holes in dark clouds. A thin line is a *ray*. Many rays together make a *beam*. Why don't you make up a word for a group of beams?

If light travels at 300,000 kilometers a second, how far can it go in one minute?

300,000 kilometers × 60 seconds = 18,000,000 kilometers a minute

Imagine how far light could travel in a year! It can go 9 ½ trillion kilometers (six trillion miles). This distance is known as a *light-year.* Three and one-third light-years make a *parsec.* How long is a parsec?

Light will keep traveling in a straight line until something stops it or changes its direction. If light hits an object that will let no light pass through, that object is called *opaque.* Can you think of something that blocks light? Does a rock? How about a soccer ball? Remember how a solar eclipse happens? The opaque moon keeps us from seeing the sun for a little time. Opaque objects make shadows by absorbing light.

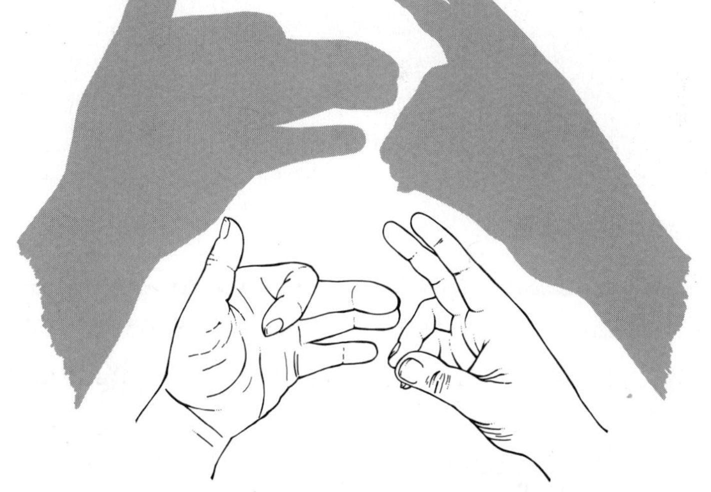

Some objects let light pass through. Such objects are called *transparent.* Look around the room. What transparent objects do you see? How would the room be different if all these objects were made opaque?

How Do We See Light?

Imagine a telescope that would be small enough to fit into your pocket, powerful enough to let you see an object several miles away, and yet able to adjust itself to show you an object two inches away. Imagine also that this telescope could repair minor damage itself, perform its own upkeep, and could not be duplicated by any science laboratory in the world. How much do you think such a wonderful machine would be worth? It would be priceless.

God has given you two such marvelous pieces of equipment—your eyes. Scientists cannot explain everything about how the eyes work. They can only describe what happens when light enters the eye.

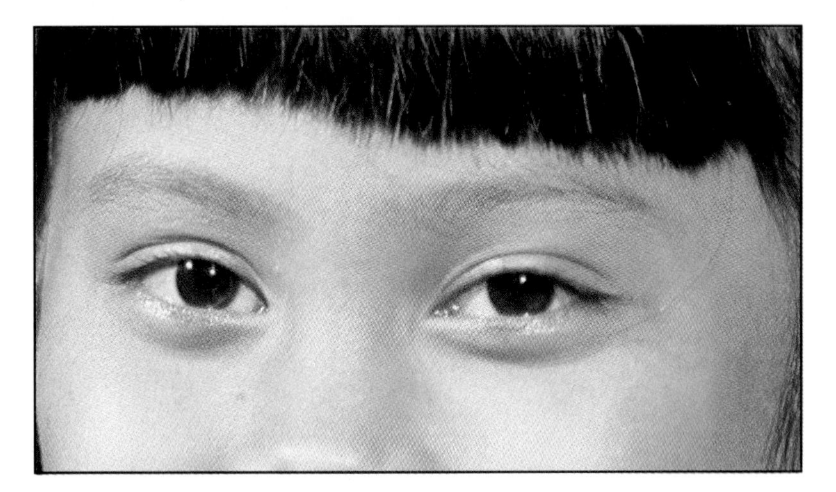

Your eyeball is a little bigger than the ball you play jacks with. It has three layers. The *sclera,* the white of the eye, keeps the shape of the eye. It is white except for a transparent part, the *cornea,* which lets light in.

The second layer is the *choroid,* a thin tissue with blood vessels in it. Part of this layer forms the *iris.* The iris is probably the part of someone's eyes you notice and remember. What part of the eye is that? The iris has

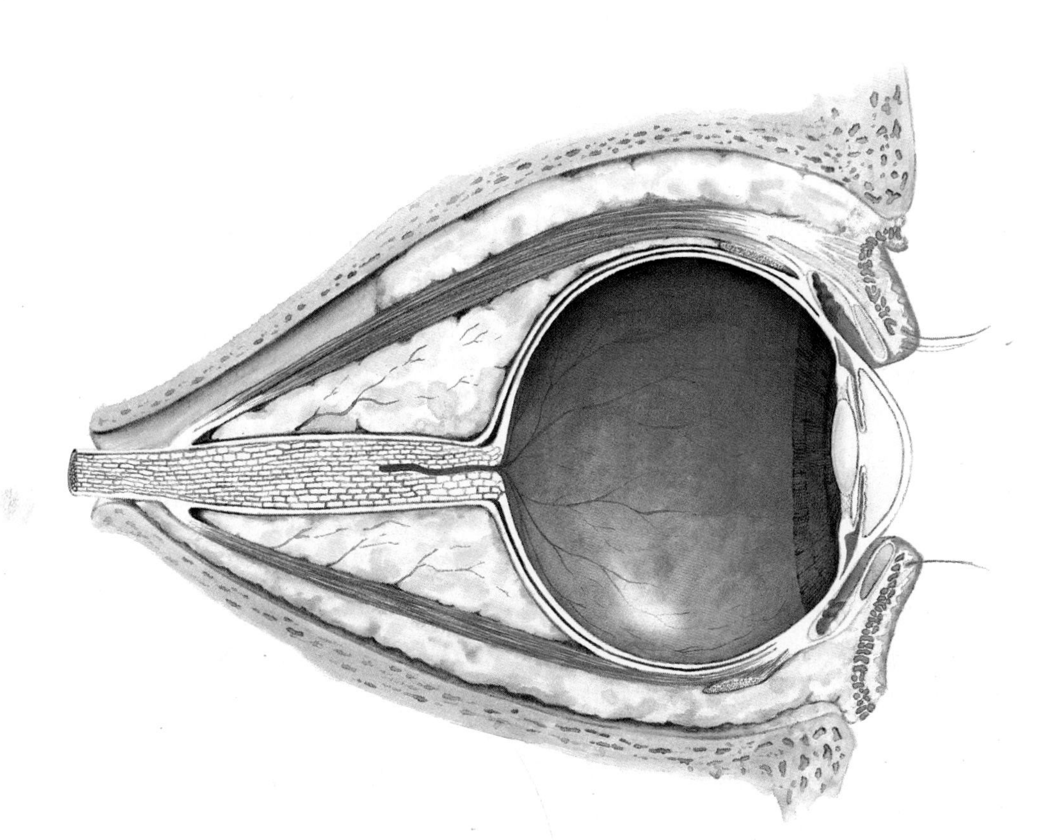

muscles that make the small opening in its center change size. If the light is bright, this opening, the *pupil,* gets small; if the light is dim, the pupil opens wide to let in as much light as possible.

The changes in the pupil protect the innermost part of the eye from getting too much light. The inside layer is the *retina.* It has thousands of *photoreceptors,* nerve cells that are sensitive to light. *Photoreceptor* comes from two Latin word parts: *phot(o)-* meaning "light," and *recipere* meaning "to receive." Can you think of some other words that have *phot(o)-* in them? What do they have to do with light?

The photoreceptors are connected to the *optic nerve* which carries nerve messages, or *impulses,* to the brain. The brain then interprets the messages.

Behind the pupil is the *lens,* a clear sac of tissue about the consistency of jello. Two muscles hold the lens and change its shape. When you look at something close, the muscles push in on the lens, making it thicker. When you look at something far away, the muscles relax, and the lens flattens out.

If the eyeball is longer or shorter than normal, then the lens cannot focus the light on the retina. The rays focus in front of the retina in a long eyeball, causing nearsightedness. In a short eyeball, the rays focus behind the retina, causing farsightedness. Glasses or contact lenses help the eyes' lenses focus light correctly.

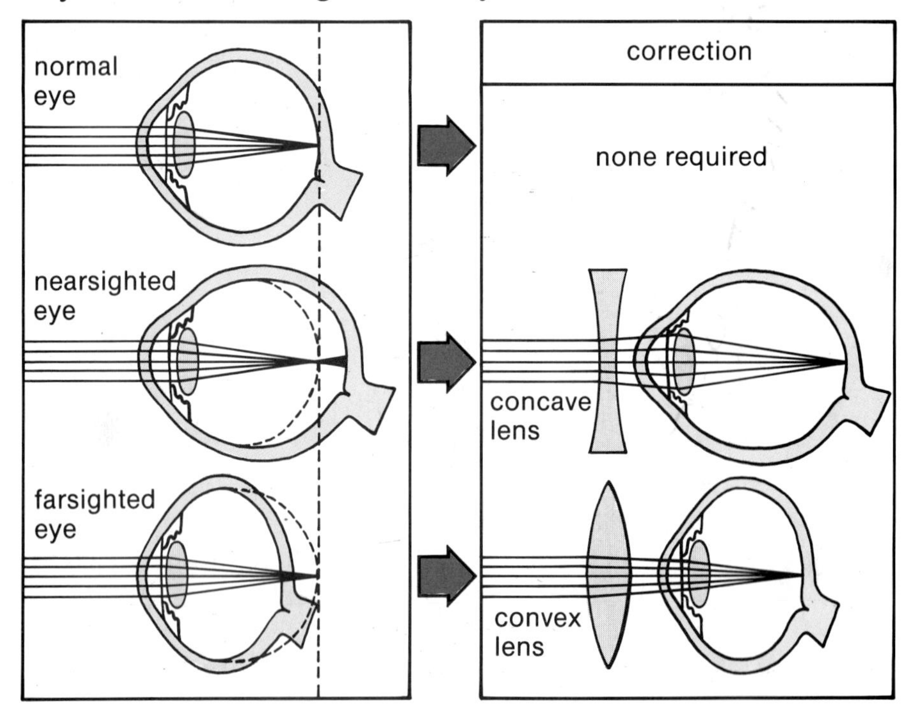

Most of the space behind the lens is filled with a clear substance something like jelly. It is called the *vitreous humor. Vitreous* comes from the Latin word for "glass"; *humor* comes from a word meaning "liquid." Why is *vitreous* a suitable description of this substance?

What Is Color?

If opaque objects keep light from passing through, where does the light go? Does it all sink into the object? When light hits an opaque object, some of the light waves sink in—are absorbed—and others are sent back to our eyes. The ones sent back are the only ones we see as color. Look around the room until you see a red object. That object looks red to you because it has absorbed all light waves except the ones that your eye sees and your brain reads as red.

What Is Not Color?

Black objects absorb most light rays. Is black a color then? Complete black is really the total lack of color. What do you suppose white, the opposite of black, is? White is all colors being reflected together.

When light strikes an opaque object, you see the reflected light as color. But what happens to the light that is absorbed? It is changed to heat. What colors would help you on cold days? What color would be best to wear on hot days?

If you have ever seen a ray of light coming in through a window or down through the trees, you probably remember it as bright and white. Is white the color of light then? Indeed, is white a color? Can there be color without light?

Light waves have color. White is a mixture of all light waves. To see color, we must see light waves reflected.

Remember the imaginary trip in space at the beginning of the chapter? The space between the stars was unlit even though the stars are putting out great light. The dark remains because there is nothing in empty space, not even enough dust, to scatter and reflect the light of all those stars.

What Reveals Color

You may have noticed when you were shining the flashlight in the dark room that you could see the beam of light. Earth's air is not nearly so free of dust and other particles as outer space is. The light waves from the flashlight bounce off particles in the air, and we can then see the beam. The dust is scattering the light waves. Sunlight that streams down through trees and in through windows also bounces off particles in the air, and so we "see" the light.

This scattering of light on dust is what makes our sky look blue and our sun look yellow. When the sun's light enters our air during the middle of the day, the wavelengths are coming down from fairly straight above. The dust in the air catches and scatters some of the shorter blue wavelengths. The sky then looks blue. The red and yellow wavelengths, being longer, pass through. So the sun looks yellow to us.

When the sun is low in the sky, the light comes in at an angle and must pass through more dust. More blue wavelengths are scattered out of the light, making the sun look orange or red. Sometimes clouds with lots of water in them absorb blue and green wavelengths. How does the sky look then? How do these facts fit with this old saying:

Red sky at night,
Sailors' delight.
Red sky at morning,
Sailors take warning.

Remember our imaginary trip in space again. Why do you think that the stars and planets seemed so bright and colorful?

Finding Out . . .

About Color

1. On a sunny day, take a prism and a piece of white paper outside or to a window.
2. Hold the prism to the light and put the paper under it.
3. Turn the prism until you can see bands of color on the paper.
4. What color shows up on the one side? What color shows up on the other side? Which color do you think has the shortest wavelength? Why?

When sunlight passes through a prism, the waves are bent and the light is broken up into bands of colors. These bands of light together make up a *spectrum.* To our eyes, the spectrum seems to have only six or seven colors. But each band in the spectrum has a huge number of different wavelengths in it. What do you think would happen to these colors if you used a second prism to bring them all back together?

Violet light has the shortest wavelength. It always appears on one end of the spectrum. Why does red appear on the other end?

Sometimes a spectrum appears in the sky. What do we call it then? What do you think is acting as a prism in the air to break up the light into its colors? Water drops can be many little prisms after a rain. How do you think you could make a rainbow appear?

Finding Out . . .

About Reflection

1. Get a flashlight and a small hand mirror.
2. In a dark room turn on the flashlight. Where does the beam hit?
3. Now hold the mirror at an angle in front of the beam. Where does the beam hit?
4. Now choose a point in the room and try to angle the mirror so that the light will be reflected to it.
5. What do you have to do to direct the light to another spot?

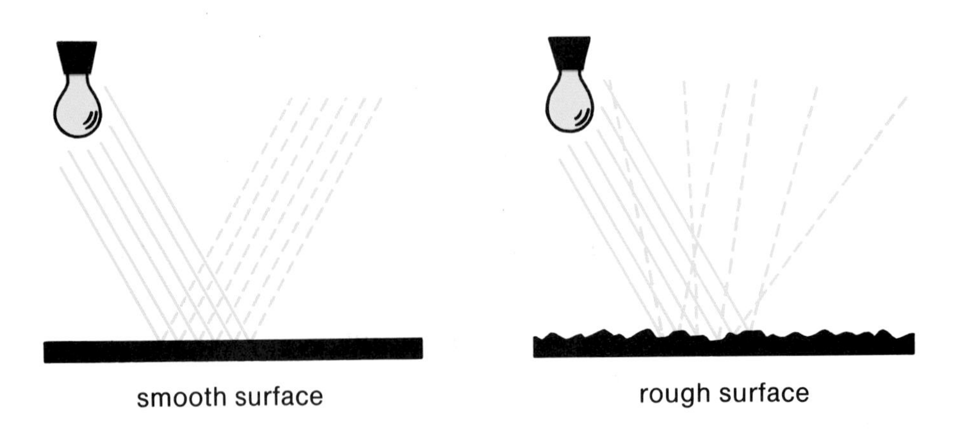

Reflection

You already have seen that some objects reflect more light than others. But some objects reflect light *better* than others. Which can you see yourself in more clearly—a puddle or a white china plate? Can you see yourself at all in a piece of notebook paper? What kind of objects can you see yourself in? What is alike about all of them?

The best reflectors are smooth, shiny, opaque objects. Polished metals like chrome and silver send light back well. Good mirrors are sheets of clear glass backed usually by silver. Light passes through the glass, but nearly all of it is sent back by the silver. When the wavelengths hit the mirror, each ray is sent back evenly with all the others. The beam, although it changes direction, keeps the same form. So the image from the mirror looks like what is in front of the mirror. If the mirror is flat and even, the reflection will be clear.

Curved Mirrors

Some mirrors are not flat. They curve in or out. Have you ever looked at your reflection on a shiny knob or a bowed window? What happens to your image? Did you ever go into a building with curved mirrors at an amusement park?

Mirrors that curve in are called *concave.* If they curve only a little, the reflection is made a bit bigger. If they curve in a lot, the image gets smaller—and turns upside down. Cars have concave mirrors on them. Can you guess where? Around the headlights. These metal mirrors help throw the light out in front of the car.

Mirrors that curve out are *convex.* Things in convex mirrors appear smaller and farther away than they would in flat mirrors. Convex mirrors take in a wider view. Where would such mirrors be useful?

Angles of Reflection

When light is reflected it changes direction, but it still travels in a straight line. Do you think, then, that you would be able to predict where a beam of light will reflect to? Yes, you can. If a light shines on a smooth, opaque surface at an angle, it will bounce off in the opposite direction at that same angle.

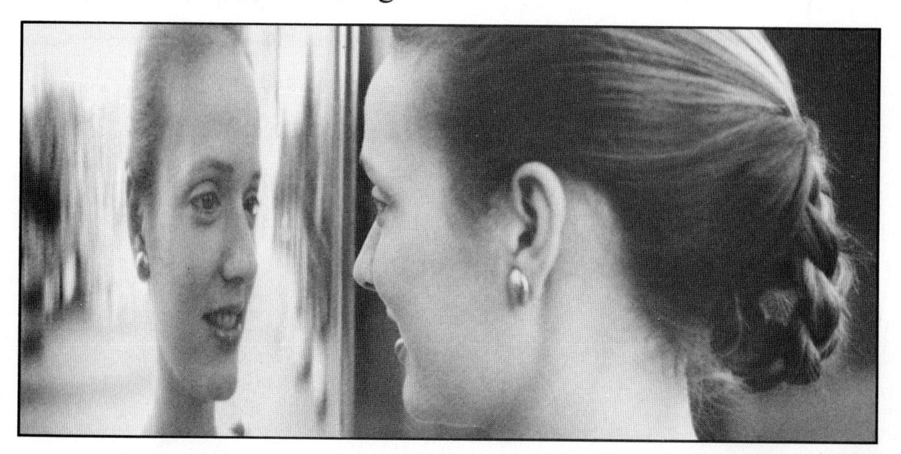

Periscopes are instruments that let you see light that is not traveling straight into your line of vision. They can, in short, permit you to see around corners or over walls. Periscopes use the facts that light always travels in a straight line and that it can be reflected. Light travels into a periscope, is reflected by a series of mirrors or prisms, and presents an image to the viewer. Soldiers in the Civil War, sailors in submarines, and sometimes hunters have used periscopes.

Name some things that do not reflect images at all. What is alike about all those objects? They are not completely smooth, are they? Even the slickest paper shows up rough under a microscope. And how many of the objects are shiny? Probably not many. So what do you think makes an object a poor mirror? Some surfaces, like snow, reflect a lot of light. But, unlike a mirror, the snow is rough and sends light back in all directions. We see all the light, but it appears as the color white, not as an image reflection.

"Yea, the darkness hideth not from thee; but the night shineth as the day: the darkness and the light are both alike to thee." *Psalm 139:12*

Machines

What do you call *work?* Carrying out the trash? Riding a bicycle? Reading this page? What qualities must an activity have for you to think that it is work?

Scientists define *work* in a way that might surprise you. They say that work is done when an object moves through a distance. Would a scientist say then that holding this book is work? No, because you are not moving anything. Is riding a bicycle work? Yes, it is. And, yes, so is picking up the trash can.

Suppose you wanted to get a treasure chest out of a deep hole. The chest weighs twenty pounds; the hole is five feet deep. What are some ways you could get the chest up?

You could jump down into the hole and try to lift the chest up. If the chest weighs twenty pounds, how many pounds of force do you think it will take to lift the chest out of the hole? If you said twenty pounds, you are right! To find out how much work you will have to do to lift the chest out, use this formula:

Amount of force × Distance = Work
20 pounds × five feet = 100 foot-pounds of work

You will have to use twenty pounds of force for five feet. But suppose you cannot lift twenty pounds over your head? You will need to find a way to use less force but still get the same amount of work done. What will have to be changed in the formula?

Let's say that you can lift ten pounds easily. How much will the distance have to be to get 100 foot-pounds of work done with ten pounds of force?

ten pounds × ? = 100 foot-pounds

You will now need ten feet. How can you increase the distance the chest has to be moved?

Simple Machines

You can use a *machine* to move the chest. Maybe you think only complicated computers, drills, and microwave ovens are machines. But a stick or a stone can be a machine. Anything that makes work easier is a machine. Machines make our work easier.

Inclined Planes

Look at the picture on this page. This is a simple machine. Where have you seen such a machine being used? It is an *inclined plane*. In this phrase, *plane* means "a flat surface." *Inclined* means "leaning, slanted." How could you use an inclined plane to lift the treasure chest out of the hole?

Have you ever seen an inclined plane holding a door open? What do we call the machine when it is being used that way?

Can you see the inclined planes in these pictures?

Pulleys

Another simple machine is a *pulley*. A pulley is a wheel with a groove around its outside. A rope passes over the pulley and fits into the groove. When you pull the rope, the pulley turns.

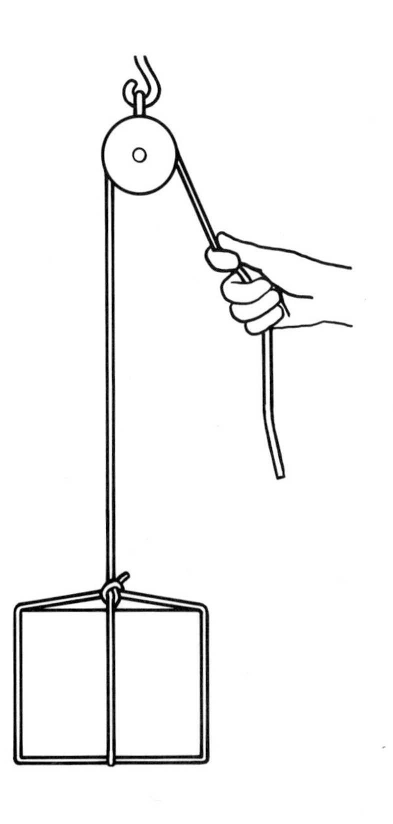

When a pulley is fastened to something that does not move, it is called a *fixed pulley*. Pulleys change the direction of force much the way mirrors change the direction of light.

Suppose that the treasure chest is in a hole that is too small for an inclined plane to be used. How could a fixed pulley help you get the chest out? How would you set the pulley up?

Sometimes pulleys are used in pairs. One pulley is fixed, and one is hooked to the object to be moved. This *movable pulley* does a different job from the fixed pulley. It multiplies force. If you use a movable pulley, you will not have to use as much force to accomplish the work.

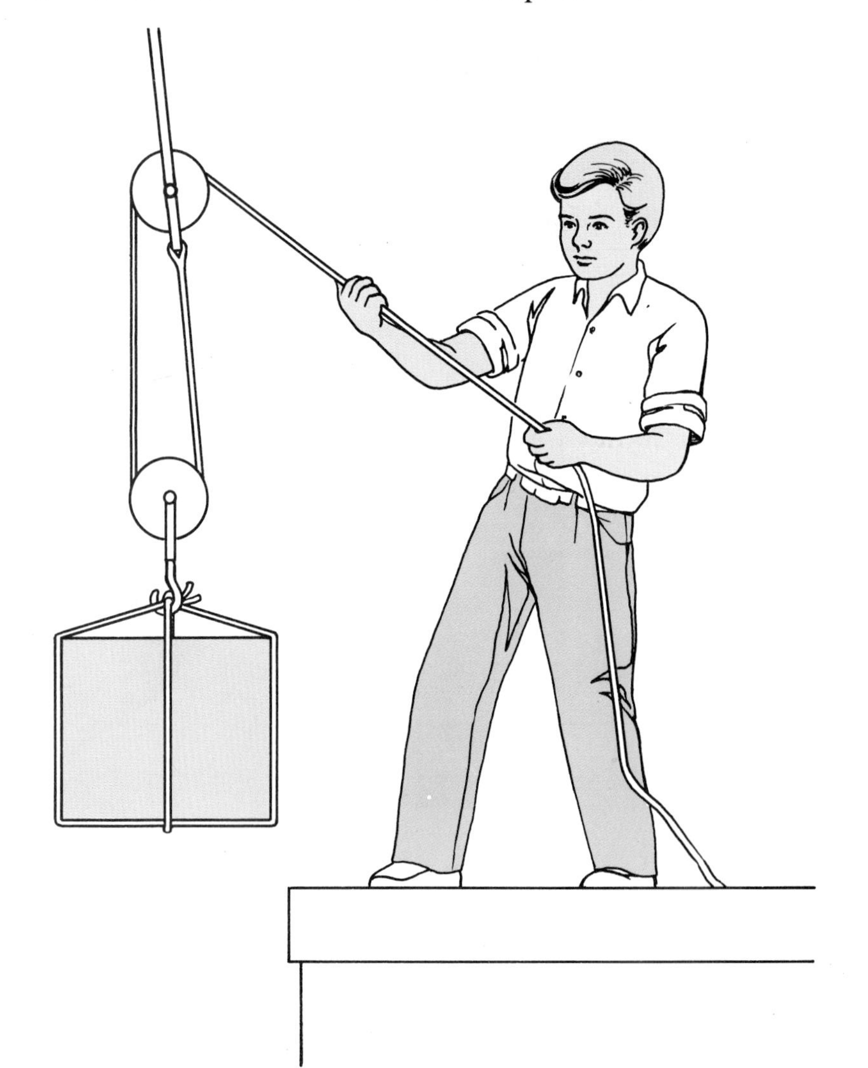

Did you know that a door knob is a machine? It is. It is a *wheel and axle.* In this machine a wheel is fixed to a shaft. When the wheel is turned, the shaft turns with it.

Look at any car on the road, and you will see three sets of wheels and axles working. Two sets carry the body of the car. Where is the third set? The driver uses it to steer.

This is a windlass. How could you use a windlass to help get the treasure chest out?

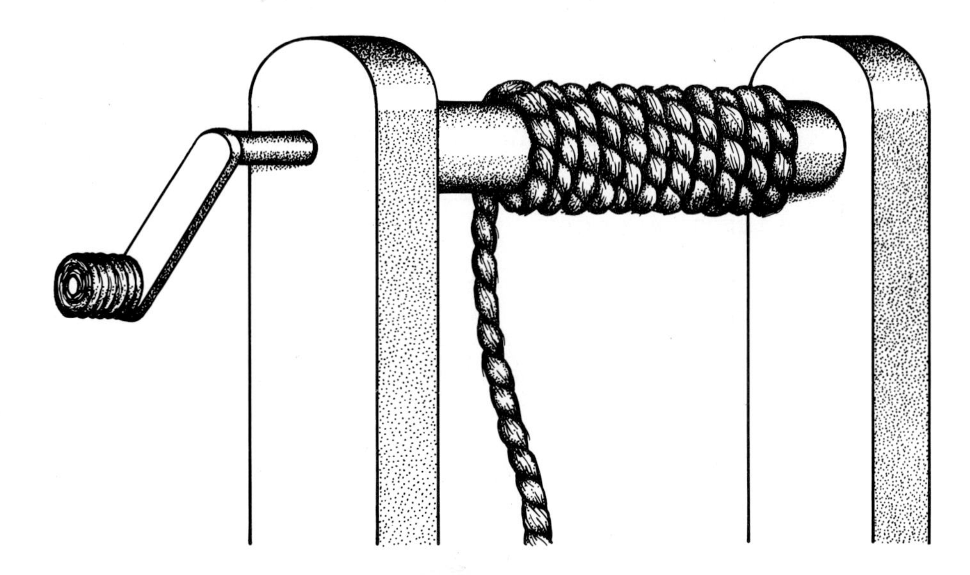

Levers

Probably the most familiar simple machine is the *lever.* Almost any pole, rod, or stick can be a lever. A lever is a bar that turns on a point.

The point on which the bar rests is the *fulcrum.* The closer the fulcrum is to the load, the easier it will be to move the load. Suppose you rigged up a pulley to lift the treasure chest. But when you jumped into the hole to tie a rope around the chest, you found that you could not get the rope under the chest. How would a lever help you?

Is this boy using a lever?

Finding Out . . .

About Levers

1. Get a spring scale, a plastic bag, gram weights, a wooden ruler, some string, and a chair.
2. Choose some weights and put them into the bag. Record how much weight is in the bag. Tie the bag to one end of the ruler.
3. Attach the spring scale to the other end of the ruler. Lay the ruler over the chair, using the back as a fulcrum.
4. Lift the bag, using the lever. Experiment by moving the fulcrum closer and farther away from the bag being lifted. When is the bag easiest to lift? Record your observations.

Wedges

Let's say that by using one or more simple machines, you were able to lift the treasure chest out of the hole. But it is sealed shut. You could wait until you get back to your house to open it. Your curiosity is too great, though. You want to open it now. Another simple machine might help.

A *wedge* is really two small inclined planes put together. Axes, chisels, and even nails are wedges. Sometimes a wedge splits an object, makes holes in it, or chips it. Sometimes a wedge can tilt a heavy object a little off the ground.

Can you think of a wedge used at the dinner table? How might you use a wedge to get into the treasure chest?

"And the house, when it was in building, was built of stone made ready before it was brought thither: so that there was neither hammer nor ax nor any tool of iron heard in the house, while it was in building." *I Kings 6:7*

Finding Out . . .

About Screws

1. You will need a sheet of construction paper, scissors, a felt marker, a ruler, and an unsharpened pencil.
2. Make a square of the paper. Lay the ruler diagonally on the paper, from one upper corner to the opposite bottom corner. Draw a line with the felt marker.
3. Cut along this line. You should have two inclined planes now.
4. Hold your pencil upright. Put the shortest side of the inclined plane along the pencil. Now, with the felt-marker line showing, wrap the inclined plane around the pencil.
5. You have made a screw. Turn the pencil around once. How far does the inclined plane rise? Record your observations.

Screws

Everybody knows what a screw is. But few may know that it really is a spiral inclined plane. The screw is not always driven into wood. Sometimes it lifts things.

An electric drill uses a screw. How? If the treasure chest is really well locked, you may have to wait until you get home and use the electric drill on it!

Trees

There are so many trees in the world that we usually do not even think about them. But imagine what your city or your neighborhood would look like without any trees at all. Can you think of any trees that you pass on your way to school? Could you describe any of the trees to someone else—or do all trees look alike to you?

You can learn to tell which group a tree belongs to and how to tell one tree from another in a group. In other words, you can learn to classify trees.

A tree is a tall plant with one long stem. Trees may be monocots, dicots, or conifers. Do you remember how the monocots and the dicots are different from the conifers? Conifers have seeds in cones; monocots and dicots have seeds in flowers and fruits.

Classifying by Leaf

You can classify trees by leaf shape and size. Be sure to look at the leaves carefully, observe the details, and notice the differences.

Do you remember what conifer leaves look like? If you do not, be sure to check that section of the book again before you start to classify trees.

Simple and Compound Leaves

Monocot and dicot leaves can be put in one of two groups: simple leaves and compound leaves. Leaves that are not divided into separate parts are *simple leaves.* Simple leaves may have *lobed* edges—parts that stick out like knobs or peaks. Lobes can be rounded or pointed. Can you find the lobed leaf below?

Compound leaves have separate parts, not merely lobes. Each separate part is called a leaflet. Look at the pictures of leaves on this page. Which leaves are simple? Which are compound? How are they different?

Finding Out . . .

About Leaves

1. Gather ten different kinds of leaves.
2. Decide whether each leaf is simple or compound. Make two groups.
3. Tell whether each simple leaf is lobed or not.

Pinnate and Palmate

There are two kinds of compound leaves—*pinnately compound* and *palmately compound. Pinnate* comes from a Latin word, *pinna,* meaning "feather." Look at this pinnately compound leaf. How do you think this kind of leaf got its name?

A palmately compound leaf has all its leaflets attached at the same point at the top of the leaf stem. It is similar to the way your fingers are attached to your hand.

Of all the compound leaves in the picture, which are palmate and which are pinnate? What do you think the Latin word *palma* means?

Plants are classified or identified with a *classification key.* A classification key is made up of paired statements. Choose the statement from each pair that describes the leaf you are studying. Follow the directions at the end of the statement you choose. Keep reading pairs of statements and following directions until you find the name of your leaf.

A Simple Classification Key to Trees

1a. Leaves needlelike or scalelike	go to 2.
1b. Leaves broad and flat	go to 9.
2a. Leaves scalelike	go to 3.
2b. Leaves needlelike	go to 4.
3a. Cones are berrylike and dark blue	Juniper
3b. Cones are woody, very large trees	Giant Sequoia
4a. Needles flattened	go to 5.
4b. Needles not flattened	go to 6.
5a. Needles 1/2 inch or less long, in two rows along stem	Hemlock
5b. Needles longer than one inch, not in two rows	Firs
6a. Needles four-sided	Spruce
6b. Needles not four-sided, needles in clusters	go to 7.
7a. Needles coming off in fall (deciduous)	Larch
7b. Needles 2-14 inches long, not coming off in fall (evergreen)	go to 8.
8a. Cones more than a foot long	Sugar pine
8b. Cones less than a foot long, needles in clusters of five	White pine

9a.	Leaves simple	go to 10.
9b.	Leaves compound	go to 21.
10a.	Leaves more round than long	go to 11.
10b.	Leaves more long than round	go to 14.
11a.	Leaves with pointed edges	go to 12.
11b.	Leaf edges smooth, leaf fan-shaped	Ginkgo
12a.	Leaves with five distinct lobes, not fuzzy on bottom of leaf	Sweet gum
12b.	Leaves without five distinct lobes	go to 13.
13a.	Leaves light green on top, fuzzy white below, 3-5 lobes	Sycamore
13b.	Leaves with several pointed lobes (more than five)	Maples
14a.	Leaves lobed	go to 15.
14b.	Leaves not lobed	go to 17.
15a.	Leaves dark green above, light green below, the lobes ending in a point	Black oak
15b.	Leaves light green, lobes are rounded	go to 16.
16a.	Leaves with three lobes, sometimes one or two; very spicy smelling when crushed	Sassafras
16b.	Leaves with many more than three lobes	White oak

17a. Leaves large, dark green, shiny, and thick	Magnolia
17b. Leaves thin, not shiny	go to 18.
18a. Leaves 3-4 times longer than width, leaves narrow	Willow
18b. Leaves 2 times longer than width	go to 19.
19a. Leaf edges with tiny teeth	go to 20.
19b. Leaf edges smooth	Dogwood
20a. Leaf tubes easily seen on leaf surface and evenly spaced, dark green on top	Elm
20b. Leaf tubes not easily seen	Cherry
21a. Leaves palmately compound	Buckeye
21b. Leaves pinnately compound	go to 22.
22a. Leaves twice pinnately compound	go to 23.
22b. Leaves once pinnately compound	go to 24.
23a. Trunk of tree has large thorns	Honey Locust
23b. Trunk of tree has no thorns	Mimosa
24a. Leaflets very long and narrow	Palm
24b. Leaflets egg-shaped	Black Locust

"For ye shall go out with joy, and be led forth with peace: the mountains and the hills shall break forth before you into singing, and all the trees of the field shall clap their hands. Instead of the thorn shall come up the fir tree, and instead of the brier shall come up the myrtle tree: and it shall be to the Lord for a name, for an everlasting sign that shall not be cut off." *Isaiah 55:12-13*

Finding Out . . .

About Trees

1. Get a small twig and a cone from an evergreen tree.
2. Using the key, try to tell what kind of conifer it is.
3. Record your observations.

12 How Earth's Crust Wears Down

"And surely the mountain falling cometh to nought, and the rock is removed out of his place. The waters wear the stones: thou washest away the things which grow out of the dust of the earth." *Job 14:18-19*

If you took a walk through southern England, you might imagine that you were walking where Alfred the Great had ridden his horses, waged his battles, and ruled his people more than a thousand years ago. In a way that is true. But in another way, you could never really walk the same hills or till the same soil that the Saxons did.

Every day wind and water change the surface of the earth. They move sand, break down rocks, wear away mountains, and carry tons of soil from one place to another. Most of the changes are slow and gradual. Some blocks of granite in Egypt have been wearing down for more than 3,000 years. But sometimes the changes are swift and devastating. A whole town in Quebec, Canada, once disappeared in a landslide in less than two hours.

Weathering

Rocks can be broken down into smaller pieces by *weathering*. Although that term may sound as though only weather changes the rocks, plants and acids can also weather stone.

Mechanical weathering happens when wind, frost, fire, water, or roots act on a rock and the rock changes. For example, wind carrying sand can etch away at a stone quickly, scouring off bits that then fly along to weather other stones.

Frost breaks up rocks. Do you know what water does when it freezes? It expands. If water seeps into the pores or the cracks in rock, what will happen when the temperature drops below freezing? Sometimes water that has run underground freezes. When it expands, it pushes up the surface and small rocks come to the top. Then a thaw comes, and soil falls under the rocks and holds them on the surface. There weathering will work on the rocks, forming more soil.

Running water can wear stone down as well. How are stones in creeks and on beaches different from stones in fields and along roadbeds?

Plants can break up rocks. How is it possible that a frail flower or a tiny seedling tree could split a rock? Roots of plants can push into a small crack in a rock and spread out. As the plant grows, its roots and stem push with steady force against the rock. After a while a small plant can expand enough to break a boulder. A plant can grow even through a city sidewalk because the power of its growth forces the cement to give way.

Forest fires heat up rocks in a way that the sun does not. A fire rushing over a rock can make the outer layer expand and split off. If the rock is surrounded by fire long enough, it can actually break apart from the heat.

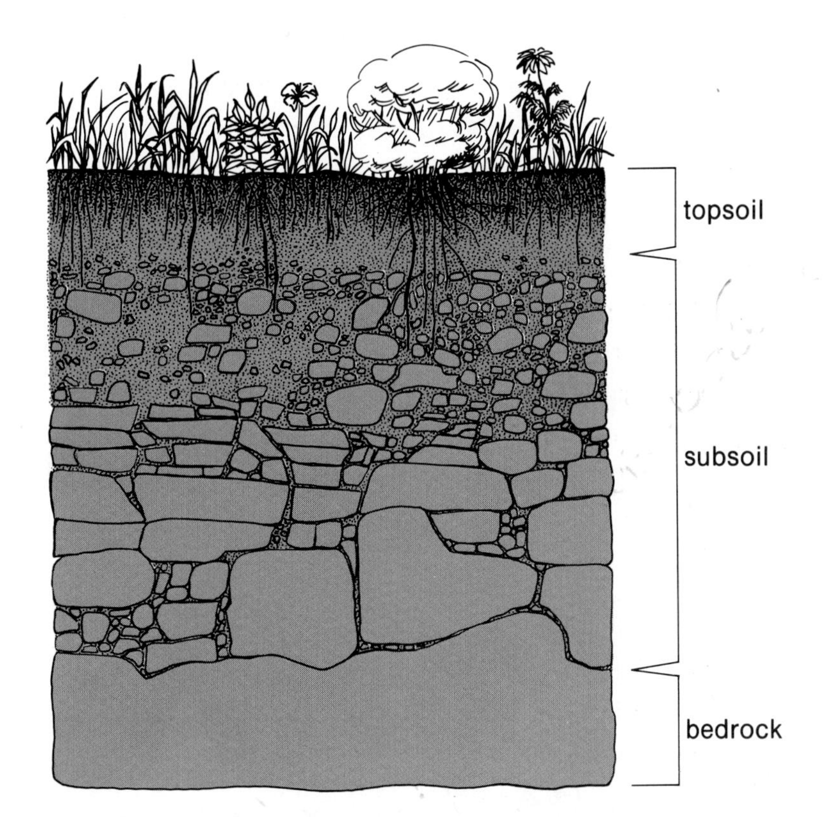

When gases like carbon dioxide mix with water, *chemical weathering* can happen. Raindrops pick up small amounts of carbon dioxide from the air. Water and carbon dioxide make a weak acid, called carbonic acid. This acid does not hurt plants or animals, but it can change limestone, dissolving it gradually. How might a miner or a scientist use this information to identify limestone?

Weathering decays the earth's crust, breaking it down into simpler elements. Eventually rocks and boulders become particles. Mixed with dead plant material, called *humus,* soil can hold water and grow new plants.

The rich soil at the surface is called *topsoil.* The soil just under that has no humus; it is called *subsoil.* Why do you think subsoil is coarser than topsoil? Below the subsoil is *bedrock,* solid, unweathered rock.

Mechanical and chemical weathering are constantly producing new soil. What would happen to farmland without weathering? Why do you think farmers find new rocks in the fields when they plow each year?

Mass-wasting

When large amounts of earth or rock slide downhill, we say the earth's crust is changed by *mass-wasting*. Mass-wasting can be slow or terrifyingly fast. But it always makes a big change in the surface of the earth.

One kind of slow mass-wasting is called *creep*. Sometimes soil slides downhill so slowly that we cannot see or feel it moving. Even the grass is not disturbed. But by and by we can see the clues of slow mass-wasting. Telephone poles tilt; fences lean; trees grow up in a curve. Why is it important for a house on a hill to have a foundation on bedrock?

When mass-wasting is swift, it is much more dangerous. A *landslide* is a sudden downhill movement of rock or soil. If the slide is made partly of ice or snow, it is an *avalanche.*

In 1881, a town in Switzerland was mining the mountain nearby. The miners worked so far into the mountain that a crack broke upward into the top. Rocks began to fall night and day, and a huge piece of the mountain began to creep down toward the town. The villagers tried to cut down the trees on the sliding part to make it lighter and perhaps to slow it down. But the effort came too late. One September morning, the whole mountain crashed down. Millions of tons of rock and soil smashed over the town at 100 miles an hour, destroying the town and killing many people.

Not all landslides are as big or as harmful. Some occur where there are no people; some move only a few tons of soil. Big or small, landslides are brought down by one force. Can you think what force that is? What force causes all things on earth to come down?

Erosion

The carrying of soil from one place to another is called *erosion.* Water and wind cause most erosion. Wind blows soil about in many directions. But water almost always runs downward to the lowest point. Why is that? What can you guess about most erosion caused by running water?

Water Erosion

Running water carries away soil in many ways. When raindrops strike the ground, they loosen and push bits of soil. This quiet work of the rain is *splash erosion.* Heavier or longer rains often run off slopes in sheets, carrying away loose soil and even small stones. What do you think this erosion is called? It is *sheet erosion.*

When running water washes away soil, it creates new landforms. Sometimes a downpour gouges a ditch, a *gully,* in the surface of the earth. If the gully continues to carry running water, it is a *rill,* a small stream. What does this line from "My Country, 'Tis of Thee" mean: "I love thy rocks and rills, Thy woods and templed hills"?

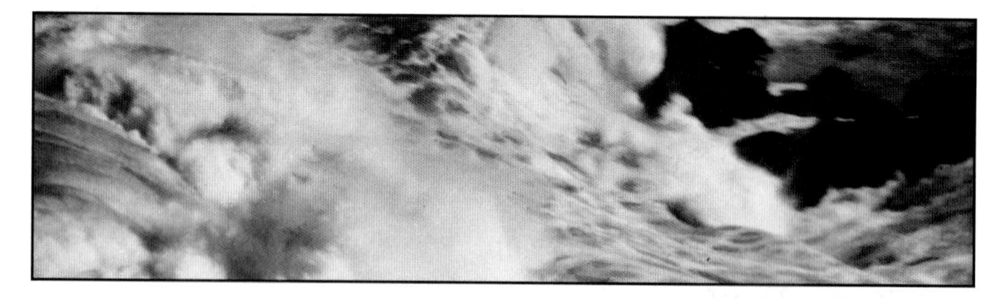

Streams, especially flooded streams, erode the surface of the earth. Rivers carve *valleys* and *gorges* and widen out their banks. How fast a valley or gorge gets worn into the crust depends on many things: how hard or soft the rock is, how much water there is, how fast the water is moving, and how long the water has been moving.

Probably the most spectacular gorge in the world is the Grand Canyon. It runs for well over 200 miles and is a mile deep in places. The sunsets blaze across the walls, turning the layers of rock orange and red. Evolutionists look at that vast canyon and at those beautiful layers of rock and say that the earth is millions of years old, that no young earth could have such a deep gorge in it.

Creationists look into the canyon and see the power of God and find evidence of the great Flood. When the Flood waters went down, they swept across whole continents with unimaginable force. The material underneath was still soft and unsettled. Under such conditions, much erosion could happen quickly. A young earth in a mighty flood would indeed have such a gorge. When the river no longer carried the huge amounts of water and the sediment hardened, erosion slowed down. The layers in the canyon walls narrow at the bottom, showing such a change in rate.

ɔicks up material, but it also lays
her places. It *deposits* soil as it slows
ne things that would cause a river to
'or the soil and other material to settle

ws into another body of water, it slows
into the other water and fans out. It
then deposits soil in a shape something like a fan. We call that triangle a *delta. Delta* is the fourth letter in the Greek alphabet. What do you think that letter looks like?

When a river floods, the water that goes over the banks slows down when it hits the land. The sediment in the water settles out, laying down a *flood plain.*

Ocean water is a powerful force for eroding the surface of the earth. The steady rushing of the waves can form cliffs, caves, and stacks.

A *wave-cut cliff* is a steep, slanted wall of earth that borders the sea. The cliffs at the Strait of Dover in southern England contain chalk. They are commonly called the White Cliffs of Dover. Do you think chalk would be easily eroded?

Sometimes the waves wear a hole in a cliff. This hole is a *sea cave.* Perhaps you have read a story about someone who hides treasure in such a place. Would that be a good place to hide treasure?

When ocean water erodes softer rock from around hard rock, a *stack* appears. Stacks are columns or towers of rock standing out of the sea. The sand and bits of rock and shell carried in seawater work like files on rock, wearing it away in the push and pull of waves.

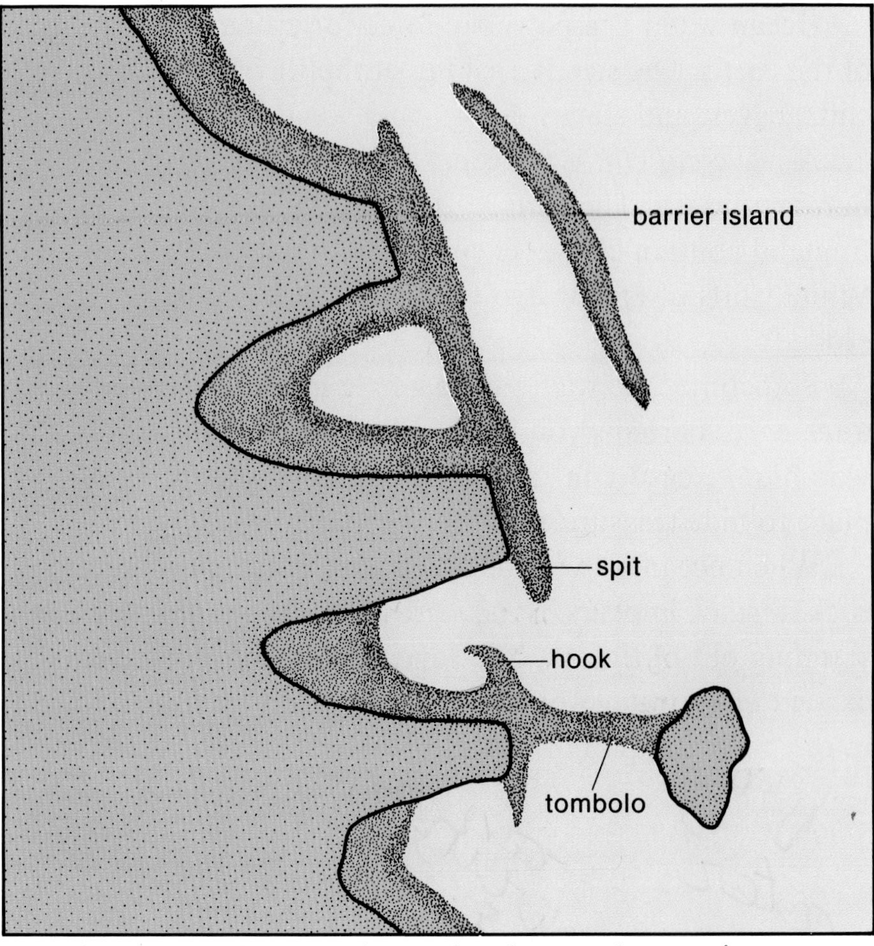

If oceans only wore down the shores, the continents might dwindle to islands after a while. God has provided for the rebuilding as well as the eroding of the earth's crust. Ocean waves wear down shores; ocean currents build them up and make other landforms in the sea.

A *spit* is a bar of sand that reaches out from an island or the shoreline. It is deposited there by the working of the ocean. A *hook* is a spit with a bend in it.

Barrier islands are sandy beaches that are not connected with the mainland. Why do you think they are called barriers? A *tombolo* is a beach of sand or gravel that connects two islands or an island and the mainland.

Frozen water also makes changes on the earth. What is one way that freezing water weathers the surface? A *glacier* is a huge mass of ice moving slowly. When snow falls on snow, and more snow falls on that, the weight forms a great block of ice. When that block gets heavy enough, it begins to move, scraping over the surface of the earth and sometimes shoving rocks and soil ahead of it. Why do you think that glaciers do not form everywhere it snows?

The new landforms gouged out by glaciers have names that sound like something out of science fiction. A *cirque* (pronounced *surk*) is a large round hollow scooped out by a glacier. When ice melts and water fills a cirque, a mountain lake called a *tarn* forms. A *fjord* (pronounced *fyord*) is an inlet from the sea that has been made deeper by a glacier. *Fjord* is a Norwegian word. Why do you think Norway has many fjords?

Glaciers, like ocean water and streams, deposit material too. The rock and soil pushed along by the *snout* or front edge of the glacier are called *till.* Ridges of till are left when glaciers melt back. *Moraines* and *drumlins* are two kinds of hills made by glaciers.

Glaciers can deposit material when they melt as well. Meltwater carries earth and rock much as a stream does. Also, when glaciers melt they send billions of gallons of water flowing to streams far below them. Meltwater is fresh water, which is water that is good to drink. God designed the glaciers to store water in the coldest months when water is not usually scarce and to release it in warmer months when streams and reservoirs are low.

Finding Out . . .

About Water Erosion

1. Get two half-gallon milk cartons, two oblong cake pans, some fine potting soil, a spoon, a sprinkling can of water, and an ice cube.

2. Cut one side out of each carton. Fill both with soil within one inch of the top. Make a "riverbed" in each carton with the handle of the spoon. Put the cartons in the baking pans. Lift one end of one carton about four inches, keeping the spout at the top.

3. Sprinkle one quart of water slowly into the top of the tilted carton. Watch what happens to the soil. Sprinkle the same amount of water into the other pan that is sitting level. What happens to that soil?

4. Now tilt the second carton and put the ice cube at the top. Let the ice cube move and melt as it will. Record all your observations.

Finding Out . . .

About Controlling Erosion

1. Get the same equipment you used for the Finding Out About Water Erosion, except you will not need an ice cube. You will also need two large measuring beakers.
2. Fill both cartons within one inch of the tops with dry soil. Put both in the baking pans and tilt both cartons.
3. "Plow" vertically in one carton and horizontally in the other, using the handle of the spoon or your fingers.
4. Then slowly sprinkle one quart of water into the vertically "plowed" soil. Watch what happens to the soil. Then sprinkle another quart of water at the same rate into the other carton. Watch what happens. Collect the run-off from both cartons separately. Which kind of plowing prevented more erosion? Record your observations.

Wind Erosion

When wind carries away loose material and hollows out a basin in the ground, it creates a *blowout.* What does the name tell about the landform?

Wind deposits sand, building up hills called *dunes.* How is the work of the wind on the earth like the work of water? How is it different?

Erosion comes from two Latin word parts that mean "to gnaw off." Why is that a good name for this process? All the wearing down of the earth is called *degeneration.* Hebrews 1:11 says the earth "shall wax old as doth a garment." The earth will eventually grow old and wear out like clothes do.

But degeneration is not the only process at work. God has also established *conservation,* ways for energy, soil, and other things to be preserved or renewed. Hebrews 1:3 tells us that God is "upholding all things by the word of his power."

Some erosion can be prevented with careful use of the land. Farmers keep soil from washing away by *contour plowing,* plowing "with the land," following the curves of the hills. Strip-cropping, in which crops are planted in bands along the contours, also slows down run-off. Rows of trees between fields also help stop wind erosion, especially during plowing.

Erosion can also be prevented with responsible methods of clearing land. Where vast areas are stripped and burned, as in the great rain forests of South America, nothing can keep millions of tons of soil from being swept away. Careful planning and cutting—rather than total destruction—can conserve soil and preserve the forests.

Shores, too, can be protected or rebuilt. *Seawalls* are barriers of steel, wood, or concrete built along the beach. Galveston, Texas, has had a seawall since 1900, when a hurricane whipped the ocean waves across the city with great destruction. The Army Corps of Engineers rebuilt part of the beach in Miami, Florida, by pumping up tons and tons of sand from under the sea.

A rich topsoil is a finer treasure than the giant sequoias that grow from it or the diamonds buried beneath it. It is the very base upon which our physical life rests. It supports the plants that provide our food and replenish our air. God has not only provided our earth with good soil, He has also established the processes by which it is renewed. If we are careless with the soil, if we do not perceive the great cycles and endeavor to operate within them, we waste one of God's best blessings to us. We are to be good stewards of this gift; we must use the soil wisely so that the earth may continue to bring forth its bounty.

"Heaven and earth shall pass away: but my words shall not pass away." *Luke 21:33*

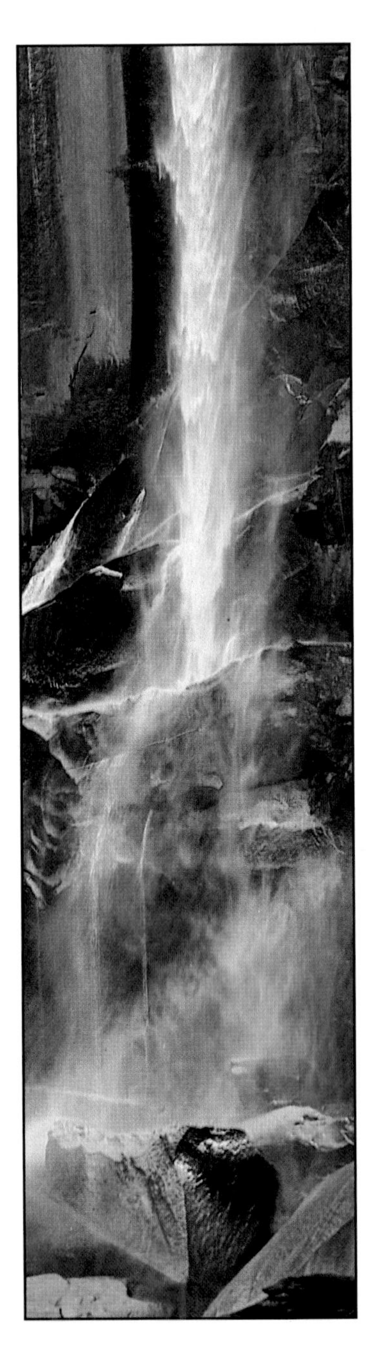

Index

Photo Credits

Cover: Suzanne R. Altizer (large), NOAA (top inset), Unusual Films (bottom inset)
Title Page: George R. Collins
Alaska Division of Tourism: 163
Suzanne R. Altizer: 21 (both), 40, 46, 57 (right), 59 (top left, top right), 61 (top), 62, 64 (top), 65 (top left, bottom left), 67 (bottom right), 71 (bottom), 72 (top right, bottom right), 76, 77 (large), 81, 82, 96, 98, 101, 131 (top left), 155, 157 (both), 161, 166, 168, 172, 173 (right), 174 (right), 177 (all), 182 (left)
Teresa Barnett: 25 (right)
Steve Black: 63 (right)
Carolina Biological Supply Company: 131 (bottom)
Brad Carper: 36, 65 (right), 91 (inset), 139 (inset), 151, 152, 162 (top left, bottom), 171 (both), 182 (right), 202
Steve Christopher: 147, 186 (left)
George R. Collins: 8, 9, 16, 17 (inset), 19 (right), 28, 39 (large), 44, 55 (both), 57 (left), 59 (bottom), 60, 70, 77 (inset), 80, 91 (large), 126 (right), 144, 150, 158, 173 (top left, bottom left), 174 (top left), 176 (both), 181, 182 (right), 183 (both), 185 (both), 190, 191, 201
Grace Collins: 195
Creation Science Foundation, Ltd., Australia: 20 (bottom), 26 (top left, top right), 35, 38 (bottom), 126 (left), 128 (all), 129 (top right)
Timothy N. Davis: 71 (top)
David Fisher: 56
J. A. Franklin: 129 (bottom)
Kenneth Frederick: 17 (large), 61 (bottom), 64 (bottom), 67 (top), 72 (left), 74 (all), 75, 174 (bottom left)
V. Ann Glenn 63 (left)
Breck P. Kent: 19 (left), 23, 24 (left), 26 (bottom), 123 (both), 124, 125 (both), 129 (top left), 130 (top), 131 (top right), 133 (both), 136 (bottom left, bottom right), 137, 138
Lick Observatory, University of California: 2, 108, 109
Steve Liverman: 27 (left)
Miriam Mitchem: 24 (right), 25 (left)
NASA: 1 (both), 4, 10, 107 (both)
NOAA: 39 (inset)
National Center for Atmospheric Research/National Science Foundation: 41
National Park Service: 73, 136 (top)
  Richard Frear: 188
  John Kaufmann: 196 (large)
New Brunswick Department of Tourism: 193 (right)
Kathleen S. Ramsey: 184
South African Tourist Corp.: 135
James Staebler: 139 (large)
U.S. Dept. of Agriculture: 20 (top), 22, 27 (right), 31, 32, 33, 38 (top), 186 (right)
U.S. Fish and Wildlife Service:
  Gary Zahm: 130 (bottom)
  John Nickels: 132
  Philip K. White: 134
Unusual Films: 13, 30, 34, 42, 47, 54, 58, 68, 69, 85, 90, 105, 106, 118, 127, 142, 153, 167, 169, 175, 197, 198
Ward's Natural Science Establishment, Inc.: 189, 192, 193 (left), 199
World Bank Photo:
  Edwin G. Huffman: 162 (top right)